T0311694

Cambridge Elements ≡

Elements in Philosophy and Logic
edited by
Bradley Armour-Garb
SUNY Albany
Frederick Kroon
The University of Auckland

LOGICAL CONSEQUENCE

Gila Sher
University of California, San Diego

CAMBRIDGE
UNIVERSITY PRESS

CAMBRIDGE
UNIVERSITY PRESS

University Printing House, Cambridge CB2 8BS, United Kingdom

One Liberty Plaza, 20th Floor, New York, NY 10006, USA

477 Williamstown Road, Port Melbourne, VIC 3207, Australia

314–321, 3rd Floor, Plot 3, Splendor Forum, Jasola District Centre,
New Delhi – 110025, India

103 Penang Road, #05–06/07, Visioncrest Commercial, Singapore 238467

Cambridge University Press is part of the University of Cambridge.

It furthers the University's mission by disseminating knowledge in the pursuit of
education, learning, and research at the highest international levels of excellence.

www.cambridge.org
Information on this title: www.cambridge.org/9781108986847
DOI: 10.1017/9781108981668

First published 2022

A catalogue record for this publication is available from the British Library.

ISBN 978-1-108-98684-7 Paperback
ISSN 2516-418X (online)
ISSN 2516-4171 (print)

Logical Consequence

Elements in Philosophy and Logic

DOI: 10.1017/9781108981668
First published online: August 2022

Gila Sher
University of California, San Diego
Author for correspondence: Gila Sher, gsher@ucsd.edu

Abstract: To understand logic is, first and foremost, to understand logical consequence. This Element provides an in-depth, accessible, up-to-date account of and philosophical insight into the semantic, model-theoretic conception of logical consequence, its Tarskian roots, and its ideas, grounding, and challenges. The topics discussed include: (i) the passage from Tarski's definition of truth (simpliciter) to his definition of logical consequence; (ii) the need for a non-proof-theoretic definition; (iii) the idea of a semantic definition; (iv) the adequacy conditions of preservation of truth, formality, and necessity; (v) the nature, structure, and totality of models; (vi) the logicality problem that threatens the definition of logical consequence (the problem of logical constants); (vii) a general solution to the logicality, formality, and necessity problems/challenges based on the isomorphism-invariance criterion of logicality; (viii) philosophical background and justification of the isomorphism-invariance criterion; and (ix) major criticisms of the semantic definition and the isomorphism-invariance criterion.

Keywords: logical consequence, logical semantics, model theory, criterion of logicality, invariance under isomorphisms

ISBNs: 9781108986847 (PB), 9781108981668 (OC)
ISSNs: 2516-418X (online), 2516-4171 (print)

Contents

1 Introduction

This Element aims at an in-depth, philosophically oriented, readable yet formally careful study of the semantic concept of *logical consequence* (henceforth, LC) – arguably, the most central concept of logic and one of the most vibrant topics of discussion in contemporary philosophy of logic. The Element seeks to get to the bottom of substantial philosophical questions concerning LC, questions that are often overlooked or taken to be unsolvable. As a result, it offers a unique perspective on LC.

1.1 The Idea of Logical Consequence

The idea of LC, or logical inference, is the idea of what follows logically from what. Given a collection of sentences $\Gamma = \{S_1, S_2, \ldots, S_n, \ldots\}$, $n \geq 0$, and a sentence, S, either S follows logically from Γ – S is a LC of Γ – or not. For example, the sentence "The number 1 has a successor" is a LC of the sentence "Every number has a successor," and the sentence "Biden won the election" is a LC of the sentences "Either Trump won the election or Biden won the election" and "Trump did not win the election." But "Every number has a successor" is not a LC of "The number 1 has a successor," and "Biden won the election" is not a LC of "Either Trump won the election or Biden won the election."

To understand the idea of LC in depth is to understand, among other things:

- In virtue of what a given sentence is a LC of another sentence (other sentences)
- What is the role of LC in knowledge
- Why and how LC works in the world (why making logical errors in, say, the design of an airplane can cause it to crash)
- What are the distinctive characteristics of LC
- What laws and principles govern or underlie LC
- Whether there is a precise method for determining that S is (or is not) a LC of Γ
- Whether there is just one kind of LC or many
- How the idea of LC relates to that of consequence in general
- What the structure of a system of LC is or could be
- What are the mathematical properties of LC (system[s] of LC)
- What is the source of normativity of LC

Logical consequence is sometimes thought to be a trivial relation, one that is obvious and cannot provide genuinely new knowledge. This view, however, is likely to be mistaken. Many mathematical theorems, which are LCs of mathematical axioms, provide genuine and indeed (at least originally) surprising new knowledge, as surprising as much of the new knowledge acquired by science.

Indeed, in science, too, logical inferences are used to arrive at far from obvious predictions and discoveries. Although here, unlike in mathematics, new predictions and discoveries are normally arrived at through a joint use of logical and nonlogical inferences, it is highly unlikely that logical inferences employed to arrive at new results do not play a substantial role.

One might object on the ground that the primitive logical rules used in such inferences are obvious or at least very simple. There is, however, nothing in the idea of logical rules that requires primitive rules to be obvious or simple: The choice of which rules to treat as primitive is largely pragmatic. More importantly, even when the primitive rules are obvious (or simple), combinations of such rules are often far from obvious.

1.2 Proof-theoretic and Semantic Approaches to Logical Consequence

The concept of LC is commonly understood both in terms of *proof* (S is a LC of Γ iff [if and only if] there is a proof of S from the sentences of Γ) and in terms of *truth* (S is a LC of Γ iff the truth of all the sentences of Γ guarantees the truth of S). Accordingly, the theory of LC has two branches: proof theory, which systematizes the notion of LC in terms of proof; and semantics or model theory, which systematizes it in terms of truth. The common proof-theoretic and semantic symbols for LC are "⊢" and "⊨," respectively. If Γ is a collection of sentences (premises) and S is a sentence (conclusion), "Γ⊢S" says that S is *logically provable* or *derivable* from the sentences of Γ and "Γ⊨S" says that the truth of the sentences of Γ, assuming that they are all true, *logically guarantees* the truth of S. In both cases, we also say that the consequence (inference) is *logically valid*.

Historically, systems of LC began as proof systems, centering on logical rules of proof such as modus ponens ($S_1 \supset S_2$, $S_1 \vdash S_2$) and universal instantiation (($\forall$x)Φx ⊢ Φa), where Φ is a formula and a is an individual constant (name of an individual). Semantics was often used in informal explanations but was not part of the logical system. Starting in the early twentieth century, however, logicians integrated the semantic account into their logical systems. Today, logical systems are usually divided into three fully developed subsystems: syntax, proof theory, and semantics (or model theory). Syntax offers a precise formulation of the language of a given logical system, proof theory offers a precise formulation of logical *provability* (or *derivability*) for that system, and semantics or model theory offers a precise formulation of LC for the given system in terms of models and truth. The term "LC" is commonly used to indicate the semantic or model-theoretic version of "following logically." In this Element we study the semantic theory of LC.

1.3 Historical Origins of the Semantic Approach to Logical Consequence

From the outset, logicians used semantic notions to explain and motivate their development of modern logic, though at first largely informally. For example, Frege, whose *Begriffsschrift* (1967 [1879]) is often used to mark the birth of modern logic, said that all of the axioms of his logical systems are *true* and its rules *truth-preserving*. The largely informal use of semantic notions continued until the publication of Tarski's semantic definition of LC (1983 [1936a]). Even Gödel's celebrated proofs of the completeness of standard first-order logic (1986 [1929]) and the incompleteness of stronger logical systems (1986 [1931], applied to logic) are of this kind. Whereas today, Gödel's completeness theorem is understood to show the extensional equivalence of the proof-theoretic and semantic notions of LC in standard first-order logic, originally it was presented as establishing the completeness of the proof-theoretic method of this logic in light of our informal understanding of logical inference/consequence in terms of truth. (By "*standard*" first-order logic, I mean, in this Element, "having the standard logical constants (ℓcs): '~,' '&,' '⊃,' '≡,' '=,' '∃,' '∀,' and ℓcs defined from these.")

Some metalogical results prior to Gödel were already formulated explicitly in model-theoretic terms (e.g., Löwenheim's 1915 [1967 (1915)] and Skolem's 1920 [1967 (1920)] theorems). And Hilbert made important contributions to the development of model theory at the turn of the twentieth century (see Hilbert 1950 [1899], Hilbert and Ackerman 1950 [1928]). Still, model theory was not an integral part of modern logic at the time. It was only after the development of the semantic definition of LC by Tarski (1983 [1936a]) that logical semantics or model theory became one of the cornerstones of modern logic, alongside proof theory.

1.4 Consequence in General and Logical Consequence

There are many kinds of consequence. For example, "*a* is a physical body; therefore, *a* does not move faster than light" is a *nomic* physical consequence. Logical consequence is a consequence relation/concept of a special kind.

The general relation of consequence – S is a consequence of Γ – is a relation of transmission or preservation of truth from Γ to S. The weakest type of consequence is:

Material Consequence (MC)
> S is a MC of Γ iff: if all the sentences of Γ are true, S is true,
>> where truth is truth *simpliciter* – that is, *material* truth in the sense of truth-in-the-actual-world.
>> In symbols: *S is a MC of Γ iff T(Γ)⊃T(S).*[1]

---

[1] "⊃" is the truth-functional conditional.

Material consequence is an extremely weak consequence. Generally, all that is required for S to be a MC of Γ is that either one of the sentences of Γ is materially false or S is materially true. Both "Tarski is a US president; therefore, Biden is a logician" and "Tarski is a logician; therefore, Biden is not a logician" are MCs. Not all consequences, however, are so weak. Nomic consequences are stronger than MCs, but there are still stronger types of consequence. Logical consequence is a stronger type of consequence. This is reflected in the traits commonly attributed to it: strong generality, necessity, formality, topic neutrality, certainty, normativity, and so on. (Nomic consequences are not formal or topic neutral and their generality, necessity, certainty, and normativity are weaker than those of LCs.) Different types of consequence are due to different types of relations between their premises and conclusion. While nomic physical consequences are due to physical relations between physical constituents of their premises and conclusion, LCs are due to logical relations between logical constituents of their premises and conclusions.

The notion of LC has been expanded to logics of multiple kinds, such as modal and relevance logics. Here we focus on the relation of LC in what is often called *predicate, formal*, or *mathematical logic*, which is the main modern successor of Aristotelian logic and is widely considered a core logic.[2] Even within the boundaries of this type of logic, however, the scope of LC is, philosophically, an open question.

1.5 Philosophical, Mathematical, and Linguistic Interest in Logical Consequence

The theory of LC is significant for several disciplines, principally philosophy, mathematics, and linguistics. In this Element I focus primarily on the philosophical character of LC as it is studied in mathematics and philosophy. For important work on issues related to LC within linguistics, see, for example, Montague (1974), May (1985), and the overview in Peters and Westerståhl (2006).

2 The Semantic Definition of Logical Consequence and Its Roots in Tarski

The semantic definition of LC has its roots in Tarski's paper, "On the Concept of Logical Consequence" (1983 [1936a]). Reading the first work in which a new theory/definition is introduced often provides important insight into the motives, goals, and considerations that led to its development. This is true of

---

[2] By calling this logic "mathematical logic," I do not mean that it is applicable only, or even primarily, to mathematics.

Tarski (1983 [1936a]). Tarski, however, disliked extended philosophical discussions, preferring to pursue mainly the formal aspects of his ideas. As a result, it is left for us to work out the philosophical content of some of Tarski's ideas and evaluate their significance.

2.1 Tarski's Route from Truth to Logical Consequence

Tarski's semantic definition of LC (Tarski 1983 [1936a]) followed upon, and extensively employed, his semantic definition of truth (1983 [1933]). This definition set out to provide a "*materially adequate and formally correct definition of the term 'true sentence'*" (Tarski 1983 [1933]: 152). By a "materially adequate" definition, Tarski meant a definition that captures the intended content of the defined concept, which, in the case of truth, he identified with the "so-called *classical* conception of truth ('true – corresponding with reality')" (Tarski 1983 [1933]: 153). By a "formally correct" definition, he meant a definition that avoids paradoxes (such as the Liar paradox) and satisfies general formal requirements on definitions.

One may wonder how a definition of truth can serve as a basis for a definition of a distinctly logical (or rather metalogical) concept such as LC, and what motivated Tarski, a mathematical logician, to define a distinctly philosophical concept such as truth in the first place. One conjecture, due to Vaught, is that Tarski's interest in truth had to do with the state of logic, and in particular metalogic, in the early decades of the twentieth century: "Tarski had become dissatisfied with the notion of truth as it was being used [in meta-logic at that time]" (Vaught 1974: 161). The notion of truth had been widely used in metalogic informally. Indeed,

> it had been possible to go even as far as the completeness theorem by treating truth (consciously or unconsciously) essentially as an undefined notion – one with many obvious properties . . . But no one had made an analysis of truth, not even of exactly what is involved in treating it in the way just mentioned . . . [T]his whole state of affairs . . . cause[d] a lack of sure-footedness in metalogic. (Vaught 1974: 161)

Vaught's point throws light on two familiar, yet quite unusual, features of Tarski's definition of truth: (i) Tarski defined truth only for *logical* languages – "formalized languages of the deductive sciences" (Tarski 1983 [1933]: 152); (ii) Tarski's definition of truth is focused on the *logical* structure (or logical content) of sentences: For each primitive ℓc – that is, a constant that determines a primitive logical structure – but not for structure-generating constants of other types (e.g., causal constants such as "because"), there is a special entry in Tarski's definition of truth that specifies the truth conditions of sentences with that logical structure. The recursive character of the definition enables it to define truth for all logically structured sentences in a finite number of steps. Given these distinctive characteristics of Tarski's definition of truth, it is not surprising that it provides a natural basis for definitions of logical, or metalogical, concepts such as LC.

Tarski classified "truth," along with "denotation" ("reference"), "satisfaction," and "LC," as *semantic* concepts. What are the distinctive characteristics of semantic concepts for Tarski? Some semantic concepts are defined in terms of other semantic concepts, for example, "truth" in terms of "denotation" ("reference") and "satisfaction." But being semantic, for Tarski, is not simply a matter of definability. His classification of concepts as semantic has to do with their *content*, and in particular with a specific aspect of their content:

> A characteristic feature of the semantical concepts is that they give expression to certain *relations* between the *expressions of language* and the *objects* about which these expressions speak. (Tarski 1983 [1933]: 252, my emphasis)
>
> We ... understand by semantics the totality of considerations concerning those concepts which, roughly speaking, express certain connexions between the expressions of a language and the objects and states of affairs referred to by these expressions. (Tarski 1983 [1936b]: 401)

Semantic concepts, thus, are not concepts that deal with just any aspect of meaning. They are concepts that deal, either directly or indirectly, with a particular aspect of meaning, namely, the *relation between language and the world*.[3]

For many concepts commonly viewed as semantic, this characterization is natural. Some of these express relations between language (linguistic expressions) and world (objects) directly. "Reference" ("denotation") and "satisfaction" fall under this category. The individual constant (proper name) "Biden" refers to the person (object in the world) Biden. The person (object in the world) Biden satisfies the 1-place predicate "x-is-president-of-the-US-in-2021," the pair of numbers $<1,2>$ satisfies the 2-place predicate "x<y," and so on. Other semantic concepts satisfy Tarski's characterization indirectly. *Truth* is such a concept. Tarski, as we have already seen, characterized his concept of truth as a correspondence concept. Truth is a property of sentences, but a sentence has this property only if a certain relation between it and the world holds. This relation, according to Tarski, is the *content* of the concept of truth, and a definition of truth is *materially adequate* only if it captures this content.[4]

---

[3] Tarski did not specify the scope of "world" ("object," "state of affairs"). I think it is reasonable to presume that he viewed its scope as fairly broad (e.g., as including mathematical objects), yet as having no definite boundaries. "World" seems to have been, for him, an intuitive, common sensical, pretheoretic notion, leaving room for a variety of precisifications.

[4] (i) Tarski also said that he reduced all semantic concepts to "structural-descriptive" concepts – concepts that belong to the "morphology" of language (Tarski 1983 [1933]: 252) and refer to linguistic expressions by describing their structure. But Tarski saw no conflict between the structural-

When it comes to the semantic concept of LC, however, Tarski's understanding of "semantic concept" is philosophically intriguing. Philosophers often think of logic as having to do with language and concepts alone, not with the world. But if LC, like truth, is a semantic concept in Tarski's sense, then it, too, has to do with the relation between language and the world. Yet how is LC related to the world? Logical consequence is a relation between linguistic entities (sentences). What in the world, or what aspect of the world, does this relation correspond to? Could we say that LC is a semantic concept because, and only because, it is defined in terms of semantic concepts, that is, concepts that have to do with the relation between language and the world, but it itself has nothing to do with this relation, and in particular with the world? Well, if the *main* concepts in terms of which LC is defined are of a kind whose *distinctive* characteristic is that they relate language to the world, then LC itself is likely to have this characteristic, and we are back to the idea that LC is a correspondence concept (of some kind). This puzzling issue requires an in-depth investigation, and we will return to it in Section 4, after we have obtained a deeper understanding of LC and related issues.

Another distinctive feature of semantic concepts, as conceived by Tarski, is that they are *metalinguistic*. To say that a concept is metalinguistic is to say that it refers to, or concerns, linguistic entities. Since semantic concepts concern linguistic entities (albeit in their relation to the world), they are metalinguistic. Given a language L, the concepts of truth and LC for L belong to its metalanguage, ML, the concepts of truth and LC for ML belong to MML, and so on.[5]

---

descriptive, that is, linguistic, definition of semantic notions and their correspondence content. Referring to the Medieval principle of *suppositio materialis* Tarski pointed out that we can express the relation between words and objects (world) linguistically, as a relation between words that refer to objects and names of (structural-descriptive expressions that refer to) these words.

(ii) Note the difference between this use of "material" and its use in Section 1.4. "Material adequacy" means "capturing the intended content of a given concept"; "material (truth/consequence)" means "truth/consequence that holds in the actual world." In this Element I use "material" in both senses. It will be clear from the context which sense is intended.

[5] Tarski's treatment of the semantic concept of truth as a metalinguistic concept has been widely criticized on the grounds that (i) it is ad hoc, (ii) it relativizes truth to language, and (iii) it diverges from natural language that has only one truth predicate. Without getting into these controversies and without referring to what Tarski himself said, let me briefly suggest responses to these criticisms that are relevant to a contemporary understanding of truth and LC. (i) It is inherent in the correspondence conception of truth that to determine whether a given sentence S is true, we need to transcend this sentence to a standpoint from which we can see (a) the sentence S, (b) its target in the world, and (c) the relation between them. This is exactly the standpoint of a Tarskian metalanguage. (ii) Tarski's definitions of truth and LC are technically relative to language, but it is significant that the entries for the *l*cs in the definition of truth are the same for all languages, and the definition of LC is also essentially the same for all languages. (iii) The natural-linguistic perspective is just one philosophical perspective on truth and LC, and not necessarily the most important one.

2.2 The Need for a Non-proof-theoretic Definition of Logical Consequence

Tarski emphasized the need for a definition of LC as it is used in everyday life, mathematics, and empirical science.[6] But by 1936 this concept already had a definition, namely, a proof-theoretic definition, one formulation of which is:

Proof-theoretic Definition of Logical Consequence

Given a logical system $\mathcal{L}$, a language L of $\mathcal{L}$,[7] a sentence S of L, and a collection Γ of sentences of L:

S is a LC of Γ iff there is a proof of S from Γ,

where a proof of S from Γ is a finite sequence of sentences, $\langle S_1, \ldots, S_n = S \rangle$, such that for every $1 \leq i \leq n$, either (i) S_i is a member of Γ, or (ii) S_i is an axiom of $\mathcal{L}$, or (iii) S_i is provable from $S_1, \ldots, S_{i-1}$ by a rule of proof of $\mathcal{L}$.

The need for a new definition of LC arose from the limitations of the proof-theoretic definition, revealed by Gödel's 1931 incompleteness theorem (1986 [1931]; see Section 4.7). This theorem shows that the proof-theoretic concept of LC is significantly narrower than the concept informally used by mathematicians and others.[8] From this, it follows that to adequately capture the full concept of LC, we need a new definition.

2.3 Fundamental Adequacy Conditions: Truth Preservation, Necessity, Formality

Tarski's paper, as I emphasized earlier, provides important philosophical insights into the semantic concept/relation of LC. These include two fundamental philosophical features of LC: *necessity* and *formality*. Tarski used these features as guidelines in his search for an adequate definition of this concept: An adequate definition must render the relation of LC both necessary and formal. The claim that LC is fundamentally necessary and formal requires a critical explanation and examination, which I will give later on. At this point, we would like to understand what Tarski himself said about these guidelines and how they constrained his definition of LC. Using "$\Gamma \vDash S$" for "S

---

[6] Although he was aware that in systematizing an intuitive, informally used concept, one cannot be completely faithful to all of its uses.

[7] In this Element, a logical system $\mathcal{L}$ has a fixed collection of ℓcs, axioms (axioms schemas), and rules of proof. A language L adds non-ℓcs to a given $\mathcal{L}$. All Ls (for $\mathcal{L}$) share the same ℓcs, axioms, and rules of proofs ($-\mathcal{L}$'s) but differ in their non-ℓcs.

[8] While the standard first-order proof-theoretic concept of LC does coincide with the intended concept when the latter is limited to standard first-order languages, the full intended concept of LC, Tarski assumed, is not limited to such languages, and as such is essentially broader. (This explanation is simpler and more straightforward than in Tarski 1983 [1936a], but the two come to the same thing.)

is a LC of Γ," we can formulate these guidelines for (or conditions on) an adequate definition of LC as follows:

> *Necessity*: An adequate definition of LC renders LCs *necessary*, that is, if Γ⊨S, then *necessarily*, if all of the sentences in Γ are true, S is true. In symbols: Γ⊨S ⊃ **Nec**[T(Γ)⊃T(S)].

> *Formality*: An adequate definition of LC renders LCs *formal*, that is, if Γ⊨S, then *formally*, if all the sentences in Γ are true, S is true. In symbols: Γ⊨S ⊃ **For**[T(Γ)⊃T(S)].

A third condition, underlying these two, is:

> *Transmission/Preservation of Truth:* An adequate definition of LC transmits/preserves *truth* (simpliciter) from Γ to S, that is, if Γ⊨S and all members of Γ are *true*, S is *true* too. In symbols: Γ⊨S ⊃ [T(Γ)⊃T(S)].

We will further discuss the third condition in later sections. Here we follow Tarski in focusing on necessity and formality.

Tarski did not provide any explanation of necessity, treating the necessity requirement as a straightforward pretheoretical requirement. He did provide a partial explanation of formality, though it is not altogether clear what the main point was. He began by saying that (i) LC is formal in the sense of being "uniquely determined by the *form* of the sentences between which it holds" (Tarski 1983 [1936a]: 414). This may lead us to think that formality, for him, was a *syntactic* feature of LC. But what Tarski said next shows that he had in mind something that goes beyond syntax: (ii) LC "cannot be influenced in any way by empirical knowledge, and in particular by knowledge of the objects to which the [sentences in Γ and S] refer" (*ibid.:* 414–415); (iii) LC "cannot be affected by replacing the designations of the objects referred to in these sentences by the designations of any other objects" (*ibid.:* 415).

Based on (iii), we may say that a definition of LC satisfies the formality requirement only if it renders LC *invariant* under uniform replacements of non-𝓁cs by constants (of the same syntactic type) that denote different objects. If we use "*" to indicate such a uniform replacement, (iii) says that the formality condition on an adequate definition of Γ⊨S is satisfied iff for every replacement * of the non-𝓁cs (of the given language), T(Γ*) ⊃ T(S*). This rendition of the formality condition naturally suggests a *substitutional* definition of LC (where "substitution" stands for "uniform replacement of non-𝓁cs"), and Tarski's next step was, indeed, to formulate, and then reject, such a definition.

2.4 Inadequacy of the Substitutional Definition

We may formulate Tarski's substitutional definition as follows:

Substitutional Definition of Logical Consequence

Let $\mathcal{L}$, L, Γ, and S be as in the proof-theoretic definition of LC. Using "$\vDash_{SB}$" for the substitutional relation of LC, we define:

> $\Gamma \vDash_{SB} S$ *iff for any uniform substitution, *, of the non-ℓcs in Γ and S by non-ℓcs of L of the same syntactic types: $T(\Gamma^*) \supset T(S^*)$, that is, if all the sentences of Γ are true under *, S is true under **

where "true" means "true simpliciter," that is, "materially true" ("true in the actual world").

Examining this definition, Tarski concluded that while it sets a necessary condition for LCs, it does not set a sufficient condition. The substitutional definition is satisfiable not just by LCs, but also by non-LCs. The reason is that whether the substitutional test works depends on the richness of the language L. If L does not have enough non-ℓcs to generate counterexamples for all non-LCs, then some non-LCs of L will be pronounced LCs by this test.

> *Example*: Let the entire nonlogical vocabulary of L consist of "Logician," "Tarski," and "Frege." Consider the consequence:
>
> (1) Tarski is a logician; therefore, Frege is a logician

Clearly, (1) is merely an MC, but it passes the substitutional test. For any uniform substitution of "Logician," "Tarski," and "Frege" by non-ℓcs of L (of the same syntactic type),

$$T[\text{Logician}(\text{Tarski})]^* \supset T[\text{Logician}(\text{Frege})]^*. {}^{9}$$

So, the substitutional test fails. The nonlogical vocabulary of L is too impoverished to provide counterexamples for all nongenuinely-LCs. Tarski concluded that the substitutional definition is inadequate:

> The [substitutional definition] could be regarded as sufficient for the sentence [S] to follow [logically] from the class [Γ] only if the *designations [names] of all possible objects* occurred in the language in question. This assumption, however, is fictitious and can never be realized. (Tarski 1983 [1936a]: 416, my emphasis)

We cannot assume that given an arbitrary language L, its nonlogical vocabulary is sufficiently rich to provide an adequate substitutional test of LC.

Another problem with the substitutional definition of LC, not mentioned by Tarski, is that generally, it takes into account only the truth of sentences in the *actual* world. Consider the consequence:

> (2) There is exactly one individual; therefore, there are at least two individuals.

---

[9] Here, [Logician(Tarski/Frege)]*=Logician*(Tarski*/Frege*).

This consequence can be expressed without using any non-ℓcs, as, for example:

(2') $(\exists x)(\forall y)x = y$; therefore, $(\exists x)(\forall y)x \neq y$.

Clearly this consequence, too, is merely material. But it satisfies the substitutional test. Since (2') has no non-ℓcs, its only substitution, *, is the identity substitution. That is, for any substitution * of the non-ℓcs of the language, the only substitutional instance of (2')'s premise/conclusion is this premise/conclusion itself. Since (2)'s premise is false in the actual world (alternatively, its conclusion is true in the actual world), it satisfies the substitutional test.

For all *: $T[(\exists x)(\forall y)x = y]^* \supset T\ [(\exists x)(\exists y)x \neq y]^*$.

Essentially the same problem can in principle arise for consequences that do contain non-ℓcs, even when there is no shortage of substitutional constants. Consider (1) once again, and assume that there is no shortage of substitutional constants. Assume further that the actual world has exactly one object. (There is no logical barrier to this assumption.) On this assumption, (1), which is only an MC, passes the substitutional test. In fact, for any finite cardinal n, if the number of objects in the world is n, there is an MC that passes the substitutional test for LCs.[10]

Another problem with the substitutional definition of LC will be noted later on, but the two we have discussed, and indeed each one separately, is sufficient to arrive at a negative conclusion about its adequacy.

> *Conclusion*: The resources available to the substitutional definition are too limited to provide an adequate test for LC. Substitution of available terms plus truth simpliciter (material truth, truth in the actual world) are not sufficient for a definition of LC.

Tarski proceeded to provide a new definition of LC – his final, *semantic* or *model-theoretic* definition. Henceforth, I will use "⊨" to name the relation of LC as rendered by this definition.

2.5 The Semantic, Model-Theoretic, Definition

The semantic definition of LC does not employ the concept of substitution at all. Instead, it introduces a new concept: "model." The definition is commonly formulated in much the same way as it was formulated by Tarski:

---

[10] For example, "There are n+1 things; therefore, Biden is a logician."

Semantic Definition of Logical Consequence (Tarski 1936)

Let $\mathcal{L}$, L, S, and Γ be as described earlier.

S is an LC of Γ – $\Gamma \vDash S$ – iff every model of Γ is a model of S.

More precisely:

S is an LC of Γ in L – $\Gamma \vDash_L S$ – iff every L-model of Γ is an L-model of S.

In Tarski's words:

> *The sentence [S] follows logically from the sentences of the class [Γ] if and only if every model of the class [Γ] is also a model of the sentence [S].* (Tarski 1983 [1936a]: 417)

An equivalent formulation is:

> *$\Gamma \vDash S$ iff there is no model M for L such that all the sentences of Γ are true in M and S is false in M.*

In symbols:

$\Gamma \vDash S$ iff $(\forall M)[T_M(\Gamma) \supset T_M(S)]$,

or

$\Gamma \vDash S$ iff $\sim(\exists M)[T_M(\Gamma) \ \& \ F_M(S)]$,

where "T_M/F_M" stands for "true/false in M."

To understand the semantic definition of LC, we need to understand the notions of model, model for L, model of Γ/S, and truth-in-a-model.

Before explaining these notions, let me attend to two issues. First, since different readers come to this Element with different backgrounds, including different terminologies and assumptions, it is important to prevent confusions by setting a unified background for explaining the notions used in the semantic definition of LC.

Linguistic–Objectual Typology

	Linguistic expressions	**Objectual correlates**
Level 0	Individual constants and variables	Individuals
Level 1	Predicates of individuals, variables	Properties of individuals
Level 2	Predicates of predicates of level 1, variables	Properties of properties of level 1

Note: (i) Individual constants denote individuals; variables of level n stand for objects of level n; predicates of a given type (level and arity [number of places]) denote properties of the same type; predicates/properties of level n+1 hold only for objects (have only arguments) of levels $\leq$n, where at least one object is of level n.[11]

---

[11] Examples: individual constant – *a*, "John"; individual – **a**, John; 1-place first-level predicate – P, "is-a-logician"; 1-place first-level property – *P*, *is-a-logician*; 1-place second-level predicate – **P**, "IS-A-NONEMPTY-PROPERTY"; 1-place second-level property – **P**, IS-A-NONEMPTY-PROPERTY.

(ii) A paradigmatic example of an individual constant is a proper name. Individuals are objects that are treated as atomic, that is, as not having an inner structure that is relevant to their semantic role.

(iii) "Predicate" and "property" range over n-place predicates and properties, $n \geq 1$. A 1-place property is a "proper property"; an n-place property, $n > 1$, is an n-place relation. Accordingly, "predicate"/"property" ranges over relations as well as proper properties. Following common conventions, an n-place function is an $n+1$ relation satisfying certain requirements.

(iv) A first-*order* system has variables of level 0, ℓcs of levels 1 and 2, and possibly non-ℓcs of levels 0 and/or 1. In *standard* first-order logic, "=" is a first-level ℓc, denoting a first-level property; "∃," "∀," and the logical connectives are second-level ℓcs, denoting second-level properties. A first-order system that includes "nonstandard" ℓcs (e.g., the second-level 1-place constant/quantifier "most") is a "non-standard first-order system," or a "generalized first-order system." "First-order system" is used for both standard and nonstandard first-order systems.

Second, three differences between Tarski's original definition of LC and the contemporary definition are:

(i) Today the background theory in which the semantic definition of LC is formulated is standard first-order set theory (ZFC),[12] while Tarski's original background theory was Russell's theory of types – a higher-order theory.

(ii) Today the semantic definition of LC is usually formulated for standard first-order consequences. Tarski himself intended the definition to apply more broadly.

(iii) Today, it is required that there be a great diversity of universes among models. For a discussion of Tarski's own view on this matter, see Hodges (1986) and Sher (1991: 40–41).

Here I use the contemporary version of Tarski's definition of LC and related notions. It is important to note, though, that in principle the definition can be formulated using different background theories. Although I will formulate the definition for standard first-order logic, it is extendable, with virtually no changes, to first-order logics with nonstandard ℓcs, as well as, with relatively small changes, to higher-order logics.

We are now ready to proceed to the notions used in the semantic definition of LC, starting with "model." A *model* is an objectual structure associated with a language, L, of a logical system, $\mathcal{L}$.

---

[12] Zermelo–Fraenkel set theory with the Axiom of Choice.

Model M for L (L-Model M)

> A model M for L is a pair $<U,\delta>$, where U is a universe and δ is a denotation
> function that assigns values in/over U to all the non-ℓcs of L. U is a nonempty
> set of individuals. δ assigns to each individual constant of L an individual in
> U and to each n-place nonlogical predicate of L, $n \geq 1$, an n-place relation on
> U (a subset of U if $n = 1$).

Note: (i) Every language L has an apparatus of models M such that for every
pair $<U,\delta>$, M=$<U,\delta>$ belongs to this apparatus.

(ii) Unlike the denotations in models of the non-ℓcs of L, the denotations
of the ℓcs of L are *not* given within models (by the denotation
function δ). They are given for all models in advance, from the
outside, so to speak, based on the fixed content of these constants.
For example, for an *arbitrary* model M=$<U,\delta>$:

(a) The denotation of "=" is the *identity* relation on U;

(b) The denotation of "∃" is the second-level property IS-NONEMPTY
(in U), so that "$(\exists x)Px$" says in M that the first-level 1-place
property $\delta(P)$ is nonempty in U, that is, that at least one individual
in U has the property $\delta(P)$;

(c) The denotation of "∼" (in contexts of the form "$\sim Pt$," where t is
a term, that is, either an individual variable or an individual
constant) is COMPLEMENTATION, so that "$\sim Pa$" says that $\delta(a)$ is in
the complement of $\delta(P)$ in U; and so on.

(iii) For the sake of simplicity, I assume bivalence, that is, there are
exactly two truth values: truth and falsehood. In Section 4 I will
explain what the choice between bivalence and nonbivalence
amounts to in connection with LC.

What, exactly, is the "job" of models in the definition of LC? What do models
need to represent, if anything, to perform their job? At this stage it is sufficient to
say that models represent certain objectual situations involving individuals and
their properties (relations) vis-à-vis a given language L. The fact that the same
non-ℓcs denote different things in different models (which represent different
situations) means that the same sentences "say" different things in different
models; the fact that all ℓcs say (essentially) the same thing in all models means
that the *logical* content/structure[13] of a given sentence in different models is
(essentially) *the same.*

---

[13] It is common to speak about the logical *structure* of sentences as opposed to their *content.*
Semantically, however, the logical structure of a sentence is also its logical content. Negation, for
example, is both (part or the whole of) the logical structure of sentences of the form "$\sim S$" *and* part
of their content.

Example: Let the nonlogical vocabulary of L consist of the individual constants *a*, *b*, the 1-place (first-level) predicate P, and the 2-place (first-level) predicate R.

Let $M_1 = <U_1, \delta_1>$, where $U_1 = \{$Frege, Tarski$\}$, $\delta(a) =$ Frege, $\delta(b) =$ Frege, $\delta(P) =$ *is-a-logician*, and $\delta(R) =$ *was-born-earlier-than*.

Let $M_2 = <U_2, \delta_2>$, where U_2 is the set of natural numbers, $\{0,1,2,3, \ldots\}$, $\delta(a) = 1$, $\delta(b) = 2$, $\delta(P) =$ *is-even*, and $\delta(R) =$ *is-smaller-than* ($<$).

Then: in M_1, "*a=b*" says that Frege is Frege and in M_2 it says that 1 is 2; in M_1, "P*a*" says that Frege is a logician and in M_2 it says that 1 is even; in M_1, "($\exists$x)R*ax*" says that Frege is was born before some person (individual) in U_1, and in M_2 it says that 1 is smaller than some natural number (individual in U_2); and so on.

Next, we turn to the definition of *truth-in-a-model*. It seems natural to define "truth-in-M" by taking a definition of truth and relativizing it to M. But not just any definition of truth will do. For example, the definition (schema) "<S> is true iff S," where "<S>" is a name of the sentence S, will not do, because this definition is blind to differences in logical structure between different sentences S.

Explanation: This essentially disquotational definition of truth does not distinguish between sentences with different logical structures (disjunctions, conjunctions, existential quantifications, universal quantifications, etc.). As such, it cannot be used to identify LCs. An appropriate definition of truth must focus on the *logical structure* of sentences. It must tell us how the logical structure of a sentence determines (participates in determining) its truth value and how different logical structures affect the truth value of sentences in different ways. Tarski's 1933 (1983 [1933]) definition of truth satisfies this requirement. As we have noted in Section 2.1, his definition focuses on the logical structure of sentences, and this makes it a suitable basis for a definition of *truth-in-a-model* (used to identify LCs).

To understand the definition of truth-in-a-model, as based on Tarski's definition of truth, we have to be familiar with two additional features of the latter definition: (i) truth is defined in terms of *satisfaction*, (ii) the definition is *recursive*.

Satisfaction. Truth bearers (here) are sentences, but often, the truth of logically structured sentences directly depends on semantic features of *subsentential* linguistic expressions. For example, the truth of "($\forall$x)Px" partly depends on semantic features of "Px." So truth for "($\forall$x)Px" is defined indirectly, in terms of a notion that applies to the subsentential expression – so-called formula – "Px". The notion of *satisfaction* is such a notion. Tarski handled this issue by incorporating a definition of satisfaction (for formulas) in his definition of truth (for sentences).

Intuitively, we can explain the notions of formula and satisfaction as follows: Formulas are expressions – both sentences and subsentential expressions – used to generate logically structured sentences. For example: the subsentential nonlogically structured formula "Px" is used to generate the logically structured subsentential formula "~Px" as well as the logically structured sentences "(∃x)Px" and "(∀x)Px"; the nonlogically structured sentence "Pa" is used to generate the logically structured sentence "~Pa"; the logically structured sentences "(∃x)Px" and "(∃x)~Px" are used to generate the logically structured sentence "~(∃x)Px ⊃ (∃x)~Px"; and so on.

The idea of satisfaction and its relation to truth are very simple. For example, the pair of individuals, <Frege, Frege> satisfies the relation "x=y," but the pair of individuals <Frege, Tarski> does not; the individuals Frege and Tarski satisfy the formula "x is a logician," Biden and the number 1 do not; the pair of numbers <2,1> satisfies the formula "x>y," the pairs <1,2> and <Frege, Tarski> do not. The connection between satisfaction and truth is straightforward. The indicated facts about satisfaction render the sentences "Frege=Frege," "Frege is a logician," "2>1," "Someone is a logician" true, and the sentences "Frege=Tarski," "1 is even," "Biden is a logician," "1>2," "Everyone is a logician" false.

Recursive Definition. There are infinitely many logical structures of sentences of L (think of "~S," "~~S," "~~~S," etc.), but the definition of truth must be finitely long. This means that it must be able to deal with infinitely many different logical structures in a finite number of steps. Tarski addressed this issue by using the *recursive* method.

The recursive method enables us to define "satisfaction" for the totality formulas (with their infinite diversity of logical structures) in a finite number of steps. This it does by showing that whether a formula with a given logical structure is satisfied by a given object (given objects) depends on whether its immediate constituents are satisfied by this (those) object(s). Since each formula is generated by a finite number of applications of ℓcs (operators) to less complex formulas and there are only finitely-many occurrences of primitive ℓcs in a formula, the satisfaction condition of each formula is determined in a finite number of steps and the definition as a whole is finitely long. (E.g., "~(Px&Qx)" is satisfied by object **a** iff it is not the case that "Px&Qx" is satisfied by **a** iff it is not the case that "Px" is satisfied by **a** and "Qx" is satisfied by **a**.)

For the recursive method to work, however, formulas have to be generated in a special way: each logically structured formula has to be generated in a *unique* way in a *finite* number of steps from "basic" ("atomic") elements. This is done by using an *inductive* definition that satisfies *uniqueness*.[14]

Formula (Well-Formed Formula or wff) of L

(i) *Nonlogically structured formulas:*

If P is a (primitive) n-place nonlogical predicate of L, n>0, and t_1, ..., t_n are terms of L (individual constants or variables),[15] *then "$Pt_1 \ldots t_n$" is a formula of L.*

(ii) *Logically structured formulas:*

(a) *If t_1 and t_2 are terms of L, then "$t_1=t_2$" is a formula of L.*
(b) *If Φ is a formula of L, "$\sim Φ$" is a formula of L.*
(c) *If Φ and Ψ are formulas of L, "(Φ&Ψ)," "(Φ∨Ψ)," "(Φ⊃Ψ)," and "(Φ≡Ψ)" are formulas of L.*
(d) *If x is an individual variable of L and Φ is a formula of L, "(∀x)Φ" and "(∃x)Φ" are formulas of L.*

(iii) *Only expressions obtained by (i) and (ii) are formulas of L.*

Here, the basic, atomic, entries are (i) and (ii)(a), and the inductive entries are (ii)(b)–(d). The formula "~(Px&Qx)," for example, is inductively uniquely generated from "Px" and "Qx" by two applications of ℓcs: & and ~, in that order.

Sentence of L

A formula of L is a sentence iff it does not have free occurrences of variables, where an occurrence of a variable x in formula Φ is free iff it is not bound by any x-quantifier (here, "∃x" or "∀x") of Φ.

Thus, "(∀x)(∃y)Rxy" is a sentence, but "(∀x)(∃y)Sxyz" is not.

We are now ready to proceed to the semantic definition of "satisfaction-in-a-model" (a relativization to models of the semantic definition of satisfaction). Before proceeding to this definition, however, we need to attend to a technical complication. Different formulas have different numbers of free variables. A formula with one free variable is satisfied by a single object, one with two free variables is satisfied by a pair of objects, and so on. How shall we state the satisfaction conditions of an arbitrary formula governed by a given ℓc regardless of the number of its free variables? Different textbooks use different techniques to overcome this technical problem. Here I use the device of "assignment-functions." Given a model M, an *assignment-function g for M* is

---

[14] An inductive definition shows how to generate a given object from basic objects by finitely-many applications of finitely-many operators. For a useful account of induction (including unique generation) and recursion in logic, see Enderton (2001 section 1.4).

[15] For the sake of simplicity, I leave out functional terms such as "the-biological-father-of" and "the-successor-of."

a function that assigns to each variable of L an individual in the universe U of M. Using this device, we say that a formula is satisfied (or not satisfied) by a given g in M.

Assignment-Function g (for L) in M

Let M=<U,δ> be a model for L.

> I. *g is a function from the set of variables of L to U. (g assigns to each variable of L exactly one individual in U, possibly the same individual to different variables.)*
> II. *g* is an extension of g:*
>> (a) *If x is a variable (of L), g*(x)=g(x).*
>> (b) *If c is an individual constant (of L), g*(c)=δ(c).*
>> (c) *If P is an n-place nonlogical predicate (of L), g*(P)=δ(P).*

Formula Φ is satisfied in M by g – Recursive Definition

Let M=<U,δ> be a model for L and g an assignment-function for L in M.

> I. *Nonlogically structured wffs*
> *If P is an n-place nonlogical predicate and $t_1, \ldots, t_n$ are terms, then "$P(t_1, \ldots, t_n)$" is satisfied in M by g iff $<g^*(t_1), \ldots, g^*(t_n)> \in \delta(P)$. (If P is a 1-place predicate, then "Pt" is satisfied in M by g iff $g^*(t) \in \delta(P)$.)*
> II. *Logically structured wffs*
>> 1. *If t_1 and t_2 are terms, then "$t_1=t_2$" is satisfied in M by g iff $g^*(t_1)=g^*(t_2)$.*
>> 2. *If Φ is a formula, then "~Φ" is satisfied in M by g iff Φ is not satisfied in M by g.*
>> 3. *If Φ and Ψ are formulas, then:*
>>> (a) *"Φ&Ψ" is satisfied in M by g iff both Φ and Ψ are satisfied in M by g.*
>>> (b) *"Φ∨Ψ" is satisfied in M by g iff at least one of Φ and Ψ issatisfied in M by g.*
>>> (c) *"Φ⊃Ψ" is satisfied in M by g iff Φ is not satisfied in M by g or Ψ is satisfied in M by g.*
>>> (d) *"Φ≡Ψ" is satisfied in M by g iff: Φ is satisfied in M by g iff Ψ is satisfied in M by g.*
>> 4. *If Φ is a formula and x is a variable, then:*
>>> (a) *"(∃x)Φ" is satisfied in M by g iff there is at least one individual **a** in U such that Φ is satisfied in M by g[**a**/x], where g[**a**/x] is obtained from g by assigning **a** to x (and otherwise leaving g the same).*
>>> (b) *"(∀x)Φ" is satisfied in M by g iff for every individual **a** in U, Φ is satisfied in M by g[**a**/x], where g[**a**/x] is as stated earlier.*

The recursive entries are II.2–4. For example, in II.2 we see how whether "~Φ" is satisfied by g depends on whether Φ is satisfied by g.

Examples: Let M_1 and M_2 be as before. That is, $M_i=<U_i,\delta_i>$ where i=1,2, $U_1=$ {Frege, Tarski}, $\delta_1(a)$=Frege, $\delta_1(b)$=Frege, $\delta_1(P)$=*is-a-logician*, $\delta_1(R)$=*was-born-earlier-than*, U_2={0,1,2,3, ...}, $\delta_2(a)$=1, $\delta_2(b)$=2, $\delta_2(P)$=*is-even*, $\delta_2(R)$=*is-smaller-than* (<).

Let g_1 and g_2 be assignment-functions for L in M_1 and let g_3 and g_4 be assignment-functions for L in M_2, where: $g_1(x)$=Frege, $g_1(y)$=Tarski; $g_2(x)$= Tarski, $g_2(y)$=Frege; $g_3(x)$=1, $g_3(y)$=2; $g_4(x)$=3, $g_4(y)$=4.

Consider the formulas "a=x," "Px," "Pb," "~Px," "($\forall$x)Px," "Rxy," and "($\forall$x)($\exists$y)Ryx."

1. "a=x" is satisfied in M_1 by g_1 iff $g_1*(a)$=$g_1*(x)$, iff $\delta_1(a)$=$g_1(x)$, iff Frege=Frege; it is satisfied in M_1 by g_2 iff Frege=Tarski.
2. (i) "Px" is satisfied in M_1 by g_1 iff $g_1*(x)$=$g_1(x) \in \delta_1(P)$, iff Frege is a logician; it is satisfied in M_1 by g_2 iff Tarski is a logician.
   (ii) "Px" is satisfied in M_2 by g_3 iff 1 is even.
3. "Pb" is satisfied in M_2 by g_3 iff $g_3*(b)$=$\delta_2(b) \in \delta_2(P)$, iff 2 is even; it is satisfied in M_2 by g_4 under the same (final) condition.
4. "~Px" is satisfied in M_1 by g_1 iff "Px" is not satisfied in M_1 by g_1, iff $g_1*(x)$=$g_1(x)$ is not a logician, iff Frege is not a logician.
5. "($\forall$x)Px" is satisfied in M_1 by g_1 iff for every $a \in U_1$, "Px" is satisfied in M_1 by g_1[a/x], iff for every $a \in U_1$, g_1[a/x](x)=a $\in \delta_1(P)$, iff every $a \in U_1$ is a logician; "($\forall$x)Px" is satisfied in M_1 by g_2 under the same (final) condition.
6. "Rxy" is satisfied in M_1 by g_1 iff Frege was born earlier than Tarski; it is satisfied in M_1 by g_2 iff Tarski was born earlier than Frege.
7. "($\forall$x)($\exists$y)Rxy" is satisfied in M_2 by g_3 iff for every $a \in U_2$, "($\exists$y)Rxy" is satisfied in M_2 by g_3[a/x] iff for every $a \in U_2$ there is a $b \in U_2$ such that "Rxy" is satisfied in M_2 by g_3[a/x,b/y], iff for every $a \in U_2$ there is a $b \in U_2$ such that $<a,b> \in \delta_2(R)$, iff for every $a \in U_2$ there is a $b \in U_2$ such that a<b. "($\forall$x)($\exists$y)Rxy" is satisfied in M_2 by g_4 under the same (final) condition.

Now, as in examples #1,2,4,6, it is often the case that an open formulas Φ is satisfied in a model M by some g (for M) but not by another. This, however, is not the case for sentences (closed formulas). If Φ is a sentence (has no free occurrences of variables), it has exactly the same satisfaction condition under all g's. The differences between different g's are not taken into account, as in examples #3,5,7. As a result, for any sentence S and model M, S is satisfied in M by some g iff it is satisfied in M by all g's.

Accordingly, the definition of *truth-in-a-model* is:

Sentence S *is true in model* M *(for* L*)*

> Sentence S *is true in M – in symbols:* $T_M(S)$ *– iff S is satisfied in M by any/ every assignment-function g. S is false in M iff it is not true in M.*

It is easy to see that "a=b," "Pa," and "($\forall$x)Px" are true in M_1 but false in M_2, "Pb" and "($\exists$x)Px" are true both in M_1 and in M_2, "($\forall$x)($\exists$y)Rxy" is false in M_1 but true in M_2, and so on.

Next, we define:

Set of Sentences Γ is true in M

Γ is true in $M - T_M(\Gamma)$ – iff every sentence of Γ is true in M.

Finally, we define the notion "model of":

Model of S/Γ

M is a model of S/Γ iff S/Γ is true in M $[T_M(S/\Gamma)]$.

We have now defined the central components of the semantic definition of LC. This definition says that S is an LC of Γ iff every model of Γ is a model of S, that is, iff in every model M for the given language L, if all the sentences of Γ are true in M, then S is true in M – $(\forall M)[T_M(\Gamma) \supset T_M(S)]$.

To determine whether a sentence S, which has a definite meaning, is an LC of a set Γ of sentences that also have definite meanings, we first *abstract* from the meanings of the non-ℓcs of S and Γ, treating them as *schematic variables* and assigning them diverse denotations in different models. We then check whether in every model M for L in which (the abstract versions of) all the sentences of Γ are true (the abstract version of) S is also true. If the answer is positive, S is an LC of Γ; otherwise, it is not.

An example of a LC based on the semantic definition is:

(3) Tarski is a logician; therefore, something (colloquially "someone") is a logician.

Using symbols to abstract from the content of the non-ℓcs of (3), we get:

(3') Pa; therefore, $(\exists x)$Px.

(3') is a (genuine) *LC because* $(\forall M)[T_M(Pa) \supset T_M((\exists x)Px)]$. Since (3) has the logical form of (3'), (3) is also a (genuine) LC.

An example of a consequence that the semantic definition of LC (rightly) categorizes as *nonlogical*:

(1) Tarski is a logician; therefore, Frege is a logician.

(1) is *not* a (genuine) LC *because* $\sim(\forall M)[T_M(Pa) \supset T_M(Pb)]$. There is a model M such that $T_M(Pa)$ and $F_M(Pb)$. One such model is:

M=<U,δ>, where
U={Tarski, Tolstoy}
δ(a)=Tarski
δ(b)=Tolstoy
δ(P)=*is-a-logician*.

We can also characterize LCs in terms of the objectual "patterns" that they represent. LCs are correlated with patterns of objects-possessing-properties-and-standing-in-relations that hold in all models, regardless of their objects. Whenever a model exhibits the pattern of an individual **a** having property P, it exhibits the pattern of P being nonempty. Whenever a model exhibits the pattern of at least one individual **a** standing in relation R to all individuals in the universe, it exhibits the pattern of each individual in the universe having at least one individual – **a** – standing to it in the relation R. The first pattern characterizes all LCs of the form (3'); the second pattern characterizes all LCs of the form

(4) $(\exists x)(\forall y)Rxy$; therefore, $(\forall y)(\exists x)Rxy$.

We are now ready to examine the adequacy of the semantic definition of LC.

2.6 Adequacy and Challenges

In this subsection we examine the adequacy of the semantic definition of LC from the perspective of Tarski's concerns and our observations.

(A) *Does the semantic definition of LC succeed in avoiding the two problems raised for the substitutional definition?*

These problems are: (a) sensitivity to the richness/poverty of the nonlogical vocabulary of a given language; (b) limited resources, in particular, limitation to a material notion of truth (truth-in-the-actual-world). These problems led the substitutional definition to classify merely MCs, such as

(1) Tarski is a logician; therefore, Frege is a logician

and

(2) There is exactly one individual; therefore, there are at least two individuals

as logical

Problem (a) does not arise for the semantic definition. Here we rely on the availability of models rather than on the availability of non-ℓcs to find counterexamples for (merely) MCs such as (1).

Concerning (b): MCs like (2), which are mishandled by the substitutional definition, are adequately handled by the semantic definition. In the case of (2), this is due to the fact that although in the actual world there is more than one individual, there are models with universes of exactly one individual, and in these models, the premise of (2) is true while its conclusion is false.

Still, so far, we have not been given enough information about models to rule out the possibility that all models share a feature that is accidental from a logical perspective and makes some non-LCs truth-preserving-in-all-models, or that there are not enough models to provide counterexamples to all non-LCs.

Tarski made at least one observation that is relevant to the latter issue. He diagnosed one of the problems with the substitutional definition as its inability to guarantee that "all *possible* objects" are referred to by expressions of L (Tarski 1983 [1936a]: 416, my emphasis). This suggests that Tarski's alternative definition guarantees that *all possible objects* are taken into account, and a natural way to guarantee this is to include all possible individuals in universes of models. But Tarski did not explicitly say what the scope of "all possible objects" is, and we have no idea what kind of possibility he had in mind. So, we still do not know whether his model-theoretic apparatus has the requisite resources for supporting a sufficiently strong notion of LC.

This leads to our next question:

(B) *Does the semantic definition of LC satisfy the adequacy conditions of necessity and formality?*

What Tarski had to establish is, in our terminology:

(i) $\Gamma \vDash S \supset$ **Nec**$[T(\Gamma) \supset T(S)]$,
(ii) $\Gamma \vDash S \supset$ **For**$[T(\Gamma) \supset T(S)]$.

That is,

(i) $(\forall M)[T_M(\Gamma) \supset T_M(S)] \supset$ **Nec**$[T(\Gamma) \supset T(S)]$,
(ii) $(\forall M)[T_M(\Gamma) \supset T_M(S)] \supset$ **For**$[T(\Gamma) \supset T(S)]$.

Does transmission-of-truth-from-Γ-to-S-in-all-models imply *necessary and formal* transmission of truth?

Tarski claimed that the answer to this question is positive. Following his formulation of the semantic definition of LC, he said: "It seems to me that everyone who understands the content of the above definition must admit that it agrees quite well with common usage" (Tarski 1983 [1936a]: 417). This meant for him that the semantic definition satisfies the *necessity* and *formality* requirements. That this is the case, Tarski added, "becomes still clearer from its various consequences. In particular, it can be *proved* on the basis of this definition, that every consequence of true sentences *must* be true, and also that the consequence relation which holds between given sentences is [*formal* in the sense of being] completely independent of the sense of the extra-logical constants which occur in these sentences" (Tarski 1983 [1936a]: 417, my emphases).

However, Tarski never spelled out the proof he alluded to. This, together with the fact that he left his conception of necessity unexplained, his explanation of formality incomplete, and the modal scope of universes of models underdetermined, suggests that he did not fully demonstrate that his definition satisfies the necessity and formality requirements. It was left for later philosophers/logicians to examine whether it does.

But this is not all. Toward the end of his paper, Tarski pointed out a problem with his definition:

(C) *Problem concerning logicality (ℓcs).*

Tarski presented this problem as follows:

> I am not at all of the opinion that in the result of the above discussion the problem of a[n] ... adequate definition of the concept of [logical] consequence has been completely solved. On the contrary, I still see several open questions, only one of which – perhaps the most important – I shall point out here.
>
> Underlying our whole construction is the division of all terms of the language discussed into logical and extra-logical. This division is certainly not quite arbitrary. If, for example, we were to include among the extra-logical signs the implication sign, or the universal quantifier, then our definition of the concept of logical consequence would lead to results which obviously contradict ordinary usage. On the other hand, ... [i]t seems to be possible to include among logical terms some which are usually regarded by logicians as extra-logical without running into consequences which stand in sharp contrast to ordinary usage. (Tarski 1983 [1936a]: 418–419)

This problem has been variously referred to as "the problem of *ℓcs*," "the problem of *logicality*," "the *demarcation* problem of logic," and so on. Here I refer to it as "the logicality problem."

The problem, as Tarski presented it, is that in the absence of an adequate criterion for, or demarcation of, *ℓcs*, the semantic definition of LC is liable to give clearly incorrect results. If we treat the standard *ℓcs* as nonlogical, it will *undergenerate:* It will classify many bona fide LCs as nonlogical. If we treat just any constant whatsoever as logical, it will *overgenerate:* It will classify many bona fide non-LCs as logical.

If, for example, we classify "=" as nonlogical, undergeneration will result. Genuine LCs, such as

(5) Pa, $a=b$; therefore, Pb

will come out nonlogical. First, there will not be a special entry in the definition of truth-in-a-model for "=," an entry that specifies its truth conditions in all models according to its (fixed) meaning. Instead, the truth conditions of identity sentences will be determined based on the general entry for 2-place nonlogical predicates. Second, there will be models in which δ assigns to "=" such relations as *is-smaller-than* (<) and, therefore, the truth conditions of "$a=b$" in such models will be: "$a=b$" is true iff $δ(a)<δ(b)$. In some of these models (depending on $δ(a)$, $δ(b)$, and $δ(P)$), the premises of (5) will be true and its conclusion false. The same thing will happen if we treat the logical connectives as non-ℓcs. In some models "⊃" will be assigned ∨ as its denotation, and as a result, many genuine LCs will be judged nonlogical.

In the opposite direction, overgeneration will result. If, for example, we classify "logician," "Tarski," and "Frege" as ℓcs, merely MCs, such as

(1) Tarski is a logician; therefore, Frege is a logician

will be come out logical. Here, the denotations of "logician," "Tarski," and "Frege" will be determined in advance, outside models, for all models, based on the actual meanings/denotations of these constants. Furthermore, these constants will be assigned specific satisfaction entries in the definition of truth-in-a-model, also based on their *actual* satisfaction/denotation. Consequently, "Tarski is a logician" and "Frege is a logician" will be true in all models.[16]

We see that without an adequate solution to the problem of logicality (ℓcs), the semantic definition of LC fails. I should note that this problem arises also for the substitutional definition of LC. If this definition treats the "wrong" constants as logical/nonlogical, over- and undergeneration result. This is the third problem with the substitutional definition we alluded to earlier, and it is questionable whether it has sufficiently rich resources to solve this problem.

The full significance of logicality, however, goes beyond what was noted by Tarski.

The "engine" of LC. The problem of ℓcs is not just a secondary, technical, problem that has to be solved before the semantic definition of LC receives the official seal of adequacy. We cannot *understand* LC *in depth* without understanding which constants, or constants of which kind, generate genuine LCs, that is, consequences satisfying the requirements of necessity and formality (or other requirements, such as generality and topic neutrality). The reason is that ℓcs are the main constituents of *logical structure*, and it is first and foremost they – their meanings/denotations – that are responsible for *logical relations* between sentences, including the *LC*-relation. This holds both for the semantic and for the proof-theoretic approaches to LC. In the former, each ℓc is assigned

---

[16] If a model does not have Tarski or Frege in its universe, some adjustment will be made, for example, Tarski/Frege will be added by fiat to its universe or the truth value of the above sentences will be determined independently of its universe.

a prefixed denotation in all models and a special entry in the semantic definition of truth/satisfaction-in-a-model, and it is these that determine whether truth is transmitted/preserved from Γ to S in all models. In the latter, each ℓc is assigned one or more rules of proof, and it is these rules that determine whether S is provable from Γ.

Not all constants can play the role of ℓcs. Under the semantic method, the constants "Tarski," "Frege," and "is-a-logician" generate material, rather than logical, consequences. And the same problem arises under the proof-theoretic method. If, instead of providing rules of proofs for constants like "is-identical-to," the proof-theoretic method provided rules for constants like "is-as-tall-as," consequences sanctioned by this method would not be genuinely logical.

Now, it is important to recognize that as far as an in-depth understanding of LC is concerned, we cannot resolve the logicality challenge by fiat or dogmatically, for example, by declaring that the only constants that generate genuine LCs are the *standard* ℓcs and the constants defined in terms of these. We cannot rule out in advance that other constants give rise to genuine *LCs*. For example, if we treat the 1-place quantifier "most," which is not definable from the standard ℓcs, as a logical quantifier, the semantic definition of LC will generate consequences that are just as logical – just as formal and necessary – as those generated by the standard ℓcs. This quantifier governs sentences that say that most things (in a given universe) have a given property, and its satisfaction condition for formulas in all models is: "'(most x)Φ' is satisfied in a model M with universe U by g iff the number of **a**'s in U for which g[**a**/x] satisfies Φ in M is larger than the number of **a**'s in U for which g[**a**/x] does not satisfy Φ in M." Under this satisfaction condition,

(6) (Most x)Px, (Most x)Qx; therefore, (∃x)(Px&Qx) (Rescher 1962)

will be classified an LC by the semantic definition. And this is as it should be. (6) is intuitively as necessary and as formal as

(7) (∀x)Px, (∀x)Qx; therefore, (∃x)(Px&Qx).

It is reasonable to expect that "most" is not the only constant of this kind.

Furthermore, we need to understand *why* – and indeed whether – the constants that are standardly considered logical are *proper* ℓcs, ones that generate genuine (formal-and-necessary) LCs.

But how do we determine which constants are logical, or even admissibly logical? In 1936, Tarski did not know how to answer this question. In fact, it was not clear to Tarski that an adequate criterion of logicality would ever be found.

Tarski left this problem altogether unresolved and, together with the open questions concerning necessity and formality, it poses a tough challenge to anyone seeking an in-depth understanding of the semantic concept of LC (and indeed, the proof-theoretic concept as well).

3 The Challenges of Necessity, Formality, and Logicality

3.1 Partial Solution to the Necessity and Formality Challenges

In a 1967 paper, Kreisel emphasized the importance of informal, intuitive concepts in constructing logical and mathematical theories. Kreisel traced his view to "[t]he 'old fashioned' idea ... that one obtains rules and definitions by analyzing intuitive notions and putting down their properties," an idea that "assumes ... that the intuitive notions are *significant*, be it in the external world or in thought" (Kreisel 1967: 138). Such significant concepts, Kreisel further claimed, are sometimes open to "informal rigour": precise analysis that decides open questions "by full use of evident properties of these intuitive notions" (Kreisel 1967: 138–139). Completeness theorems, in particular, he viewed as useful for informal rigor.

One concept used by Kreisel to demonstrate his point was the concept of LC. He claimed that at least in the context of standard first-order logic we can show that this concept receives a rigorous analysis by its semantic definition. Granting that LC is tantamount to preservation-of-truth-in-*all-structures*, Kreisel said that we need to demonstrate that there are enough *models* to represent *all* structures (so that preservation-of-truth-in-*all-models* is sufficient for LC). This, he claimed, can be demonstrated based on the completeness theorem of standard first-order logic (Gödel 1986 [1929]). There are several ways to proceed with this demonstration. One of the simplest is:

(a) By examining each of the (finitely many) axioms (axiom schemas) and primitive rules of proof of standard first-order logic, we confirm that each axiom is intuitively logically true and each rule is intuitively logically truth-preserving.

(b) We conclude that the *proof-theoretic* definition of LC provides a rigorous analysis of the intuitive concept.

(c) Based on the *completeness theorem* of standard first-order logic – $\Gamma \vdash S$ iff $\Gamma \vDash S$ – we conclude that the *semantic* definition of LC also provides rigorous analysis of the intuitive concept.

Unlike Tarski, Kreisel did not set precise adequacy conditions on a rigorous definition (for him, rigorous analysis) of LC. But we can easily adjust the above demonstration to show that the adequacy conditions of necessity and formality are satisfied. We do this by expanding step (a) to a confirmation that each of the standard first-order logical axioms and rules of proof is, intuitively, both necessary and formal.

This demonstration, however, has obvious limitations. First, it is limited to standard first-order LCs. Second, it does not enlighten us about the types of necessity and formality – or, for that matter, the intuitive scope of "all structures" – that are relevant to LC. Third, it rests on intuitive judgments about particular cases (the axioms and primitive rules of proof of standard first-order logic), a method whose reliability is in doubt. To arrive at a general, "in principle," theoretical, solution to the challenge of necessity and formality, we need a different approach.

Such an approach was taken by Sher (1991). This approach integrates the solution to the necessity and formality challenges with the solution to the logicality challenge, treating these challenges as closely interconnected. Before proceeding to these solutions, however, we ought to say something about methodology.

3.2 A Note on Methodology

Given the basicness of logic, discussions of foundational issues concerning it face serious methodological obstacles: circularity, infinite regress, lack of a basis for solving problems, and so on. To discuss the problems of logicality, formality, and necessity with impunity, therefore, we need a philosophical methodology that is capable of sidestepping these obstacles. Traditionally, it has been taken for granted that the only methodology for solving foundational problems is the so-called *foundationalist* methodology. This methodology is based on the principles that (i) our body of knowledge has a hierarchical structure; (ii) this structure has an absolute base, consisting of minimal elements of the hierarchy; and (iii) each element in the hierarchy is, and can only be, founded based on elements lower than it in the hierarchy. Eventually, then, all elements are grounded in those constituting the base. Today, it is widely recognized that the foundationalist methodology is self-defeating: Since all nonbasic elements are ultimately founded on elements in the base, the correctness of the basic elements is crucial for the correctness of all other elements. This means that providing a genuine foundation for the basic elements is essential for providing a genuine foundation for our body of knowledge as a whole. At the same time, it is structurally impossible to provide a genuine foundation for the basic elements, since the only way to provide a genuine foundation for any element, according to the foundationalist method, is to found it on lower elements in the hierarchy. But structurally, no element in the hierarchy is lower than the basic elements. Therefore, it is impossible to provide a genuine foundation for the basic elements, hence for any element in our body of knowledge.

Now, this problem is especially intractable when it comes to solving foundational problems concerning logic. The reason is that logic is universally considered a basic discipline, and therefore it is in principle impossible to provide an informative foundation for logic or solve, in a non-question-begging manner, foundational questions concerning logic. This, indeed, is a common view, encouraging a purely pragmatist approach to logic. Substantive solutions to the foundational challenges of logicality, necessity, and formality appear to be impossible. But in fact, they are not. The apparent dilemma "either you accept the foundationalist methodology or you cannot provide a foundation for logic" is a false dilemma. There is an alternative foundational methodology, *foundational holism* (Sher 2016, chapters 2 and 9).

What is foundational holism? "Holism" means different things to different people. Foundational holism conceives of our body of knowledge as composed of distinct units that are connected both to the world and to each other in a variety of ways. As such, it enables us to provide informative explanations, including explanations of foundational issues, without being subject to the rigid requirements of foundationalism. Foundational holism is naturally represented by the *Neurath-boat* metaphor, a metaphor (originally introduced by Neurath and made famous by Quine) of our body of knowledge as a boat in the sea. The foundationalist believes that when we come upon a problem – there is a hole in the boat – we can take the boat to solid ground – the base of the foundationalist hierarchy – fix the hole, and then go back to sea. But the holist regards the idea of solid ground as an illusion. To solve a problem – to fix a hole in the boat – we remain at sea, move to a part of the boat that is relatively intact and, using resources available to us on the boat, fix the hole as best we can. Once the hole is temporarily fixed, we resume our journey, obtain new knowledge, find and/ or create new resources, and refix the hole.

Some philosophers regard Neurath-boat as representing a coherentist methodology. All we can aim at is coherence with the rest of our beliefs. Foundational holism rejects this approach. Neurath-boat is a vessel on an expedition, a Beagle or a Victoria, whose task is to study the external sea and its environs (the world). Knowledge is knowledge of the world, broadly understood, but there is no Archimedean standpoint. To cognitively reach the world, we start from where we stand, use available tools, employ our critical and creative faculties, and begin, or continue, theorizing. Theorizing typically involves back-and-forth movement. Starting from elements we have, we develop new elements and then use these elements (together with others we discover or develop along the way) to reexamine the elements we started with, replace, revise, or keep these elements, and go on. Incorporating knowledge from various fields is *par de course*. Partial circularity is also *par de course*.[17] This is the way progress in theorizing is achieved by humans, and this is the way foundational questions concerning logic can in principle be solved.

We are now ready to present an intertwined solution to the challenges of logicality, formality, and necessity.

3.3 General Invariantist Solution to the Logicality Challenge: The Isomorphism-Invariance Criterion

The integrated solution to the logicality, formality, and necessity challenges starts with a search for a *criterion of logicality*, guided by the requirement that it gives rise to *consequences* that are both *necessary* and *formal*. This approach was pursued in Sher (1991), where the underlying question was:

> What is the widest notion of a *logical term [constant]* for which the Tarskian definition of "logical consequence" gives results compatible with (C1) [the necessity guideline] and (C2) [the formality guideline]? (Sher 1991: 44)

Originally, however, the criterion that offers a positive answer to this question was not developed with this question in mind. It was developed in a way that is very common in mathematics: by a generalization of earlier developments. This began with Mostowski's (1957) generalization of the standard first-order logical quantifiers, ∀ and ∃, which led to a general criterion for logical quantifiers of their type, namely second-level 1-place predicates. The second step, a general criterion of logicality for constants of all types, was made, independently, by Lindström (1966) and Tarski (1966/1986). Lindström further generalized Mostowski's generalization; Tarski arrived at his criterion from an altogether different direction, by generalizing Klein's (1872) *Erlangen Program* in geometry. (Tarski's generalization was presented in a 1966 lecture that was largely unknown until

---

[17] By "*partial* circularity" I mean circularity that concerns only few elements used in the account (so the account is largely noncircular). Furthermore, even this limited circularity may be removed at a later stage, employing the Neurath-boat method.

its publication in 1986, but later became quite influential.) All of these generalizations led to similar (if not fully identical) criteria.

It is significant to note, however, that all of these criteria – Mostowski's, Lindström's, and Tarski's – were completely detached from the semantic notion of LC and the logicality problem raised by its semantic definition. Even Tarski's lecture did not refer back to his 1936 paper (1983 [1936a]). Moreover, in his 1966 lecture, Tarski explicitly disavowed any connection between his treatment of ℓcs and the search for a general understanding of the nature of logic: "Let me tell you in advance that in answering the question 'What are logical notions?' ... I shall not discuss the general question 'What is logic?' ... [Nor shall I] be concerned ... with the problem of logical truths [LCs]" (Tarski 1966/ 1986]: 145). Questions like "What is logic?" are better left for philosophers to discuss.

Since in this Element our interest in a general criterion of logicality centers on its connection to the concept of LC (and with it, the general question "What is logic?"), we will present this criterion as it was developed with this connection in mind, based on Sher (1991 and later works).

To explain the philosophical motivation for this criterion, we take a functional approach. We start with the functional question: "What is the 'raison d'être' or function (role, task) of logic (theory of LC)?" And we focus on the epistemic dimension of this question: logic's function in the human pursuit of knowledge. Observing that humans aim at *true* knowledge of the world (knowledge of the world as it in fact is) yet are set back by limitations and obstacles of various kinds, it is clear that we greatly benefit from having a powerful method of inference (consequence), one that enables us to obtain new knowledge based on the knowledge we already have. Such a method transmits *truth* from sentences whose truth we already know to sentences whose truth we do not yet know in all fields of knowledge – that is, *universally* – and with an *especially strong force.* What kind of force? It is here that we arrive at the requirement of necessity. The method in question transmits truth from sentences to sentences "in principle," that is, in a way that is not dependent on the contingencies of our actual situation, i.e., necessarily. Whence formality? Formality, as we will see shortly, ensures that LC transmits truth (i) systematically and (ii) with an especially strong modal force.

Now, one idea that is common to the criteria of logicality developed by Mostowski, Lindström, and Tarski is the idea of *invariance.* What is invariance? Offering my own understanding, let me start with invariance in general, not specifically in logic. In its simplest form, invariance is a binary relation:

X is invariant under Y.

Intuitively, to say that X is invariant under Y is to say that X does not "notice," does not "pay attention" to, is "blind" to, is "immune" to, or is not "affected" by changes of type Y. It "abstracts" from such changes. An example from physics: The laws of special relativity (X) are invariant under changes of inertial reference-frames (Y). They are the same in all such frames. They are indifferent to, hence not affected by, replacements of one inertial frame by another.

There are many types of invariance, according to what X and Y are. The invariance used to resolve the logicality problem takes X to be a *property* and a change of type Y to be a *1–1 and onto replacement of individuals* (within and across domains). We may call invariance of this kind "property-invariance." Here "X is invariant under Y" means "Property X is invariant under all 1–1 and onto replacements of individuals (within and across domains)." When I talk about *invariance* in this Element, I usually mean property-invariance in this sense.

To understand property-invariance, we begin by noting that properties in general are *selective* in character. They "pay attention to," "are attuned to," "notice," "discern" *some* differences between individuals, but *not* others. Accordingly, they *distinguish* between *some* individuals yet *not all*. For example, the first-level property *is-a-human* distinguishes between Tarski and Mount Everest, but not between Tarski and (Meryl) Streep or between Everest and the number 1. You can replace Tarski by Streep or Everest by 1 and the property *is-a-human* will not notice. But if you replace Tarski by Everest (or 1), it will. This can be expressed in terms of "invariance": *is-a-human* is *invariant* under replacements of Tarski by Streep and of Everest by 1, but *not* under replacements of Tarski or Streep by Everest or 1. And in general, for any 1-place first-level property P, P is *invariant* under all replacements of individuals that have P by individuals that have P and individuals that do not have P by individuals that do not have P, but not under any replacement of individuals that have P by individuals that do not have P (and vice versa).

This is easily generalized to n-place first-level properties, n>1 (see later), as well as to higher-level properties. For the latter, consider the 1-place second-level property IS-A-GEOLOGICAL-PROPERTY. This property does not distinguish between different individuals that have (first-level) geological properties. It also does not distinguish between different individuals that do not have geo-logical properties. But it does distinguish between individuals that have and individuals that do not have geological properties. Thus, IS-A-GEOLOGICAL-PROPERTY does not distinguish between any two mountains (individuals that have the first-level property of being a mountain), any two canyons, any mountain and canyon, and so on. Nor does it distinguish between any two humans, any two numbers, any human and number, and so on. But it does distinguish between mountains and humans, mountains and numbers, and so on. In terms of invariance, this second-level property is invariant under some replacements of individuals but not under others. This extends to properties of any level and arity.[18]

In this way, we can sort out properties in general according to their invariances. However, if we want to identify the invariances of properties accurately, we cannot limit ourselves to replacements of *actual* individuals. Differences in selectivity between properties that have the same actual extension (e.g., *has-a-heart* and *has-a-kidney*) will be invisible if we limit ourselves to actual individuals. Furthermore, even in other cases, we need to take into account counterfactual individuals in order to understand the selectivity of properties. Consider *has-a-mass* (some mass, one or another). The selectivity of this property depends on its satisfaction conditions, and these do not distinguish between actual and counterfactual physical individuals. (Thus, to get the selectivity/ invariance of this property right, we have to realize that if Earth had a second moon, *has-a-mass* would not have distinguished between it and its actual moon.)

At this stage in our discussion there is no need to determine the exact scope of counterfactual individuals or use any special apparatus to speak about them. We simply speak about actual and/or counterfactual individuals, or more shortly *actual-counterfactual* individuals, in the intuitive, common-sensical, pretheoretical sense, without restricting their scope. By "individuals," we henceforth mean "actual-counterfactual individuals." (Later on we will say more about the scope of actual-counterfactual individuals as it pertains to logic.)[19]

We are now ready to define the notion "property P is invariant under replacement-function **r**."

P is Invariant under r – INV(P,r):

> *Informal Version.* For any property P, domain of individuals D, an argument (or an n-tuple of arguments), β, of P in D, and a replacement-function **r** on D (where the range of **r** is D'),
> *P is invariant under r*
> *iff*
> *β has the property P in D iff the image of β under r has the property P in D'.*

> *Precise Version:* Let D_1, D_2 be *domains* – nonempty collections of actual-counterfactual individuals. Let **r** be a *replacement-function –*

---

[18] Readers may wonder why the invariance applicable to second-level properties is invariance under replacements of individuals rather than under replacements of first-level properties. The answer is that our task is to distinguish between *logical* and *nonlogical* properties, and for various reasons, the former is, but the latter is not, suitable for this task. (For relevant points see fns. 20, 24, 25.)

[19] If you wonder whether mathematical individuals are actual or counterfactual, this depends on one's understanding of such individuals, and it does not affect the present discussion. (For a relevant approach to mathematical individuals, see Section 4.6(c).)

a *1–1* function from D_1 *onto* D_2 (possibly $D_1=D_2$). We will say that **r** is *indexed* to $<D_1,D_2>$.

To make the definition of "P is invariant under **r**" – "INV(P,**r**)" – as clear as possible, I focus on three simple cases:

*Case 1: P is a 1-place first-level property; **r** is a replacement-function indexed to $<D_1,D_2>$.*

$$INV(P,r) =_{Df} (\forall x)(\forall y)[[x\in D_1 \ \& \ y\in D_2 \ \& \ y=r(x)] \supset (Px \equiv Py)].$$

To speak more concisely, we can treat **r** as indexed to a single domain, D, in which case, the second domain is the (exact) range of **r**. We then define:

$$INV(P,r) =_{Df} (\forall x)[x\in D \supset (Px \equiv P(r(x)))].$$

*Case 2: P is an n-place first-level property, n> 1; **r** is as above.*
Using the concise style:

$$INV(P,r) =_{Df} (\forall x_1) \ldots (\forall x_n)[<x_1, \ldots, x_n>\in D^n \supset$$
$$[P(x_1, \ldots, x_n)\equiv P(r(x_1), \ldots, r(x_n))]].$$

*Case 3: **P** is a 1-place second-level property of 1-place first-level properties; **r** is as stated earlier.*

$$INV(P,r) =_{Df}(\forall P_D)[P(P_D) \equiv P(r^*(P_D))],$$

where:
(a) P_D is the extension of the (first-level) property P in D.
(b) $r^*(P_D)$ is the image of P_D under **r**.[20]

The full definition of INV(P,**r**) for any P (of any level and arity) is a natural extension of these partial definitions.

Examples:

P_1: *is-human*
P_2: *is-identical-to* (=)
P_3: IS-A-GEOLOGICAL-PROPERTY
P_4: IS-A-NONEMPTY-PROPERTY (IS-NONEMPTY)

D_1: {Tarski, Everest, 1}
D_2: {Streep, Grand-Canyon, 2}

r_1, r_2 are indexed to $<D_1,D_2>$
r_1(Tarski)=Streep, r_1(Everest)=2, r_1(1)=Grand-Canyon
r_2(Tarski)=2, r_2(Everest)=Grand-Canyon, r_2(1)=Streep

It is easy to see that:
  (i) P_1 is invariant under r_1 but not under r_2.[21]
  (ii) P_2 is invariant under both r_1 and r_2.[22]

---

[20] Note that while **r** is a replacement of individuals of D, **r*** is a replacement, *induced* by **r**, of first-level properties restricted to D (P_D's). The fact that **r** (a function on individuals) induces **r*** (a function on first-level properties) means that we can determine the invariance of second-level properties by focusing on individuals.

[21] r_1 assigns humans to humans and nonhumans to nonhumans; r_2 does not.

[22] This follows from the fact that both **r**'s are 1–1 functions.

(iii) $\mathbf{P_3}$ is invariant under $\mathbf{r_2}$ but not under $\mathbf{r_1}$.[23]

(iv) $\mathbf{P_4}$ is invariant under both $\mathbf{r_1}$ and $\mathbf{r_2}$.[24]

Maximal Invariance. Every property is invariant under *some* 1–1 and onto replacement(s) of individuals. This is trivial, since every property is invariant under the *identity* replacement of individuals, that is, replacement of each individual by itself. But many properties are also invariant under nontrivial replacements, as we have just seen. Are any properties invariant under *all* replacements? We have seen that *not all* properties are. For example, *is-a-human* and IS-A-GEOLOGICAL-PROPERTY are not, and it is easy to see that most of the properties that are relevant to everyday life, science, and philosophy are not. Yet some properties *are* invariant under all replacements. No matter what individuals in what domains you replace by each other in a 1–1 and onto manner, satisfaction (or possession) of these properties is not affected. These properties do not "notice" the difference between any individuals, actual or counterfactual. They are properties of a very special kind. They may pay attention to some things (which we will later identify), but only to things that are completely independent of "who" (what) are the individuals involved. We will say that these properties are *maximally invariant*. We define:

Maximal Invariance

   P is maximally invariant iff $(\forall r)$(P is invariant under r).

   In symbols:

   Max-INV(P) iff $(\forall r)$INV(P,r).

The distinctive feature of maximally invariant properties, namely, not distinguishing between *any* individuals, has long been identified as characteristic of logic.

> [G]eneral ... logic ... treats of understanding without any regard to difference in the objects to which the understanding may be directed. (Kant 1929 [1781/1787] A52/B76)

---

[23] D_1 has three individuals, so there are (up to extensional equivalence) eight distinct first-level properties restricted to D_1 (P_{D_1}·s). Since geological individuals have geological properties and nongeological individuals do not, the only first-level geological properties on D_1 and D_2 are, extensionally, the P_{D_1} {Everest} and the P_{D_2} {Grand-Canyon}. (For simplicity, I leave $\varnothing$ out.) The image of {Everest} under r_2 is {Grand-Canyon}. That is, the image of each first-level geological property restricted to D_1 under r_2 is a first-level geological property restricted to D_2, and the image of each nongeological first-level property restricted to D_1 under r_2 is a nongeological first-level property restricted to D_2. This is not the case with r_1.

[24] This follows from the fact that both r's, being functions, cannot take us from an individual to nothing or from nothing to an individual. (In contrast, 1–1 and onto functions on properties can take us from a nonempty property to an empty property.)

> [P]ure logic ... disregard[s] the particular characteristics of objects. (Frege 1967 [1879]: 5)

> [Logical] quantifiers should not allow us to distinguish between different elements of [the universe]. (Mostowski 1957: 13)

It is easy to see that all of the properties denoted (or definable) by the standard ℓcs are *maximally invariant* and all the paradigmatic examples of nonlogical properties (e.g., *is-Tarski*, *is-a-logician*, IS-A-GEOLOGICAL-PROPERTY) are not maximally invariant. For the former, take, for example, *identity* and NONEMPTINESS (the existential-quantifier property). Earlier, we saw that they are invariant under both r_1 and r_2, but in fact they are invariant under *all* r's.[25] The same holds for UNIVERSALITY (the universal-quantifier property: IS-UNIVERSAL-(in-a-given-domain)), COMPLEMENTATION, INTERSECTION, UNION, INCLUSION – the negation-, conjunction-, disjunction-, and conditional- properties in predicative formulas (e.g., "~Pt"), EXACTLY-TWO (definable from the standard ℓcs), and so on.

To bring our discussion in line with the logical and philosophical literature, let me indicate that *maximal invariance* is commonly called "invariance under isomorphisms" (Sher 1991) and "invariance under bijections" (Bonnay 2008). We have:

Maximal-Invariance ≈ Invariance under all bijections ≈ Invariance under all Isomorphisms

> P is *maximally invariant* iff
> P is *invariant under all bijections*, iff
> P is *invariant under all isomorphisms (is isomorphism-invariant)*.

Both historically and philosophically, the notion of invariance under (all) isomorphisms is especially significant. I will now offer an independent definition of this notion, starting with the notion of *structure* (as it is used here):

Structure

> *A structure **S** is a pair, <D,β>, where D is a nonempty set of individuals and β is an individual in D, an n-tuple of individuals in D (n> 1), a k-place property of individuals in D (k>0), extensionally represented, or an m-tuple of any of the above (m>1).*[26]

---

[25] For the reasons noted in fns. 22, 24. Note that while the second-level property IS-NONEMPTY is invariant under all replacements of individuals, it is not invariant under all replacements of first-level properties. Specifically, it is not invariant under replacements of nonempty properties by empty properties. This is one reason we need replacements of properties to be induced by replacements of individuals.

[26] Readers may wonder about the relation between structures (as used here) and models. Well, all models – <U,δ> – are structures – <D,β>, but not the other way around: Structures need not be associated with a language (β can be purely objectual, not associated with a specific vocabulary), and when they are, the language need not be limited to constants that are predetermined to be nonlogical.

Examples:

  (i) $<N, 1> = <\{0,1,2, \ldots\},1>$ is a structure (but $<N,-1>$ is not a structure).
  (ii) $<N, \textit{smaller-than}> = <N,\{<0,1>,<0,2>,<1,2>, \ldots\}>$ is a structure.
  (iii) $<D = \{\text{Tarski, Tolstoy}\}, \textit{is-a-logician}> = <\{\text{Tarski, Tolstoy}\}, \{\text{Tarski}\}>$ is
      a structure.

Isomorphism (of Structures)

An isomorphism of structures $S_1 = <D_1,\beta_1>$ and $S_2 = <D_2,\beta_2>$ is a 1–1 and onto function (bijection) r from D_1 to D_2 such that $r^*(\beta_1) = \beta_2$, where $r^*(\beta_1) = r(\beta_1)$ if β_1 is an individual; otherwise, $r^*(\beta_1)$ is the image of β_1 under r. If there is an isomorphism of S_1 and S_2, we say that S_1 is isomorphic to S_2 and symbolize this by "$S_1 \cong S_2$."

Examples:

  (i) $<N,1>$ is isomorphic to $<N,2>$ as well as to $<P,2>$ (where P is the collection
      of positive integers: 1,2,3, . . .), but it is not isomorphic to $<N, <1,2\gg$ or to
      $<R,1>$ (where R is the collection of real numbers).
  (ii) If D={Tarski, Tolstoy}, then $<D, \textit{is-a-logician}>$ is isomorphic to $<D,$
      is-a-novelist$>$, but it is not isomorphic to $<D, \textit{is-a-human}>$.

If $S_1 \cong S_2$, we say that S_1 and S_2 are structurally the same.

We now turn to a special kind of structure, which is relevant for *invariance under isomorphisms.* First, we define:

An Argument β of Property P in Domain D

If P is an n-place property, n>0, and D is a domain, then:

  (a) If P is a first-level property, then any n-tuple of individuals in D is an
      argument of P in D.
  (b) If **P** is a second-level property of m first-level properties of arities
      $i_1, \ldots, i_m$, then any m-tuple of first-level properties P_D of arities
      $i_1, \ldots, i_m$ is an argument β of P in D.[27]

Examples:

Let D = {**a,b**}

  (i)   The arguments in D of 1-place first-level properties P (*is-a-logician,*
      is–identical) are **a,b**.
  (ii) The arguments in D of 2-place first-level properties R (*is-identical-to*
      (=), *is-taller-than*) are $<$**a,a**$>,<$**a,b**$>,<$**b,a**$>,<$**b,b**$>$.
  (iii) The arguments in D of 1-place second-level properties **P** (IS-NONEMPTY
      ($\exists$), the 1-place MOST, IS-A-GEOLOGICAL-PROPERTY) are $\varnothing$,{**a**},{**b**}, {**a,b**}.

---

[27] A 1-tuple of individuals/properties is an individual/property.

Next, we define:

Structure for a Property P

If P is a property, D is a domain, and β is an argument of P in D, then S=<D,β> is a structure for P.

Examples:

Let D, P, R, and **P** be as in the earlier examples. Then:

(i) The D-structures for P are <D,**a**>, <D,**b**>.

(ii) The D-structures for R are <D,<**a**,**a**≫, <D,<**a**,**b**≫, <D,<**b**,**a**≫, <D,<**b**,**b**≫.

(iii) The D-structures for **P** are <D,∅>, <D,{**a**}>, <D,{**b**}>, <D,{**a**,**b**}>.

We are now ready to define "invariance under (all) isomorphisms":

Invariance under (all) Isomorphisms

Property P is invariant under (all) isomorphisms iff: for any two isomorphic structures for P, S_1=<D_1,$β_1$> and S_2=<D_2,$β_2$>, $β_1$ has the property P in D_1 iff $β_2$ has the property P in D_2.

Informally:

Property P is invariant under (all) isomorphisms iff P does not distinguish between any two isomorphic structures for P, <D_1,$β_1$> and <D_2,$β_2$>. That is, $β_1$ has P in D_1 iff $β_2$ has P in D_2.

With this we can formulate the general solution to the logicality challenge. Following McGee (1996) and Feferman (1999), this solution is sometimes referred to in the literature as "the Tarski–Sher thesis" (Tarski 1966/1986, Sher 1991).

General Solution to the Logicality Challenge
Criterion of Logicality for Properties (Tarski–Sher Thesis).

A property is logical iff it is invariant under all isomorphisms (it is invariant under all bijections, it is maximally invariant).

Examples:

Logical properties: =, COMPLEMENTATION (~), INTERSECTION (&), UNION (∨), INCLUSION (⊃), EQUIVALENCE (≡), NONEMPTINESS (∃), UNIVERSALITY (∀), EXACTLY-TWO, 1-place and 2-place MOST, FINITELY-MANY, UNCOUNTABLY-MANY, IS-WELL-ORDERED, IS-WELL-FOUNDED.

Nonlogical properties: *is-Tarski, is-Frege, is-a-logician, is-human,* IS-A-GEOLOGICAL-PROPERTY, IS-A-CAUSE-OF.

Significance of "P is a Logical Property" under the Tarski-Sher thesis.
"P is a logical property" signifies that P is an *admissible candidate* for a denotation of an ℓc in systems of predicate/mathematical logic (not that P is, or must be, the denotation of some ℓc in every such system).

Remark on the Tarski and Sher Sides of the Tarski–Sher Thesis. Technically, the Tarski and Sher versions of the thesis differ in that Tarski is widely understood to have advocated a somewhat weaker criterion than Sher, namely, invariance under *permutations* (automorphisms)[28] instead of invariance under *isomorphisms*. It is an open question whether Tarski really meant the weaker type of invariance (Tarski often assumed a background setting that is different in various ways from the one[s] used today). Be that as it may, it is important to realize that invariance under permutations (as it is understood today) is a flawed version of invariance under isomorphisms. The problem with permutation-invariance can be seen in the following example (a variation on McGee 1996). Consider the second-level property WOMBAT-NONEMPTINESS (w), defined by: for any 1-place first-level property P, w(P) iff P is nonempty (behaves like ∃) in domains with wombats and universal (behaves like ∀) in all other domains. This property is clearly not maximally invariant, since it is *not blind* to differences between wombats and nonwombats, but it satisfies the permutation version of the criterion. WOMBAT-NONEMPTINESS, however, does not satisfy the isomorphism-invariance criterion. The Tarski–Sher thesis advocates isomorphism- (rather than permutation-)invariance as a criterion of logicality.

Philosophically, Tarski and Sher were motivated by different interests. In particular, Sher, but not Tarski (see discussion earlier in this section), was motivated by the question "What is logic?" and the problem of logicality as it pertains to the semantic definition of LC. This is a significant difference. It is partly reflected in the fact that the general (invariantist) solution to the problems of necessity and formality (Section 3.4) is based on Sher rather than on Tarski. Further discussion of "What is logic?" will be given in Section 4.

Extension of the Logicality Criterion from Properties to Predicative Constants. Both Lindström (1966) and Tarski (1966/1986) formulated their versions of the criterion for objectual entities. We have already formulated the logicality criterion for objectual entities (specifically, *properties*). Sher (1991) formulated her version of the criterion for linguistic entities.

Criterion of Logicality for (Predicative) Constants (Sher 1991)[29]

(Predicative) constant C is logical iff

    (a) C denotes a property, P, of the same level and arity as C, and

---

[28] Permutation: 1–1 function p from D onto itself. Induces an isomorphism of structures with the same domain (automorphism).

[29] (i) For the sake of greater clarity, this formulation includes some redundancies. (ii) The original formulation applied also to individual-constants ("Tarski"). The present formulation applies to individual-constants through predicates ("is-identical-to-Tarski"). Either way, no individual constant is logical.

(b) *The denotation of C is defined in advance for all domains of actual-counterfactual individuals, hence for all models, and*

(c) *C is a rigid designator; its denotation is defined by an extensional function and is identified with its extension,*[30] *and*

(d) *The denotation, P^C, of C is invariant under all isomorphisms (of structures for P^C), that is, P^C is an isomorphism-invariant property and as such it behaves in the same way in all isomorphic structures within and across models.*

Examples of ℓcs and non-ℓcs: quotation names of the logical and nonlogical properties in the examples above.[31]

Expansion of the Logicality Criterion to Sentential Connectives. While structures for predicates/properties are structures of individuals and properties, structures for sentential constants are structures of (something like) states-of-affairs. We extend the logicality criterion to such constants by replacing structures of the former kind by structures of the latter kind (Sher 2016: 278–279). The atomic elements of the former structures are *individuals*; those of the latter are *atomic states-of-affairs* (correlates of atomic sentences). The invariance criterion of logicality for predicates/properties is based on replacements of individuals, that of sentential connectives/operators – on replacements of atomic states-of-affairs.

Now, in predicate/property-structures, each atomic element (individual in the domain) either has or does not have a given property.[32] In sentential-structures, each atomic element (atomic state-of-affairs) is either *the case* or *not the case*. We may symbolize this by "+" and "–." Accordingly, the correlate of isomorphism-invariance (invariance under all 1–1 and onto replacements of individuals that preserve properties) is invariance under all 1–1 replacements of atomic states-of-affairs that preserve + and –.

Criterion of Logicality for Sentential Constants (Sher 1991, 2016)

Sentential constant C is logical iff it denotes an operator, O, which is invariant under all 1–1 replacements, r, of atomic states-of-affairs that preserve + (being the case) and – (not being the case), that is, iff: $(\forall r)[O(s_1, \ldots, s_n)$ is + iff $O(r(s_1), \ldots, r(s_n))$ is +].

---

[30] Clarifications: (i) ℓcs are rigid designators in an especially *strong* sense: they have the same denotation in all formally possible domains/universes (see below), including those that are physically or metaphysically impossible.

(ii) The logicality criterion is *not* concerned with the way we *grasp* the meanings of ℓcs (MacFarlane 2015). This is due to the fact that it is designed to solve a problem (adequacy of the semantic definition of LC) that is not concerned with *grasping-conditions*.

(iii) Identifying ℓcs with their extension does not obliterate differences in the way (and number of steps in which) they denote a given extensional property; for example, "∃" and "~∀~."

[31] Further examples: Section 6.1.

[32] Or induces the having or not having of a given higher-level property by lower-level properties.

This criterion is equivalent to the usual *truth-functionality* criterion of logicality for sentential connectives. Accordingly, it does not take into account domains of individuals.[33]

Note: In predicate logic, the sentential connectives appear in two forms: as *sentential* constants – for example, "&" in contexts of the form "S_1&S_2" – and as predicative constants – for example, "&" in contexts of the form "Px&Qx" and "Px&Qy." In the former context, "&" denotes a truth-function; in the latter, it denotes ∩ and × (Cartesian product), respectively. The two versions of "&" come together in the semantic definition of truth-in-a-model, where the truth-conditions for sentences governed by logical connectives can be formulated in two equivalent ways. Consider the sentence "Pa&Qa." The two versions of its truth-condition in a model M=<U,δ> are: (i) "Pa&Qa" is true in M iff both "Pa" and "Qa" are true in M; (ii) "Pa&Qa" is true in M iff $\delta(a) \in \delta(P) \cap \delta(Q)$. Clearly, (i) and (ii) are equivalent.

To simplify the discussion, I refer to both the property/predicate and operator/connective versions of the logicality criterion as "the isomorphism-invariance criterion" (treating operators as properties). This leads to a crisp general solution to the logicality challenge:

General Invariantist Solution to the Logicality Challenge

> *A property/constant is logical iff it is isomorphism-invariant.*

Our next task is to evaluate this solution.

Evaluation of the General Invariantist Solution to the Logicality Challenge. To solve the logicality challenge in a general way, the isomorphism-invariance criterion has to categorize all and only properties/constants that give rise to *necessary and formal* consequences as logical. More specifically, the adequacy of the solution depends on whether for any selection of ℓcs satisfying the isomorphism-invariance criterion, all consequences sanctioned by the semantic definition of LC are formal and necessary. As we will see later, the answer to this question is in principle positive.

3.4 General Invariantist Solution to the Necessity and Formality Challenges

A general solution to the necessity and formality challenges has to do three things: First, it has to explain how necessity and formality enter logic in the first

---

[33] In contrast, Lindström (1966) treated sentential connectives as n-place quantifiers of a special kind, defined over domains of individuals. This is technically convenient, but philosophically, it introduces a factor that is not relevant to connectives – individuals. In so doing, it renders logical connectives nontruth-functional. (Thus, Lindström sanctions a logical connective that behaves like & in domains with κ_1-many individuals and like ∨ in domains with κ_2-many individuals, where $\kappa_1 \neq \kappa_2$ but Sher does not.)

place. Second, it has to explain the content of the formality and necessity requirements for an adequate definition of LC, in particular, which kinds of formality and necessity are required. Third, it has to show that the semantic definition of LC satisfies the formality and necessity requirements when the isomorphism-invariance criterion of logicality is used. We have attended to the first task, in part, in Sections 2.3 and 3.3, and we will further attend to it in Section 4. The second and third tasks are the subject of the present section. Essentially, the solution to the challenges of necessity and formality is based on connections between (A) logicality (isomorphism-invariance) and formality, (B) formality and an especially strong type of necessity:

A. *Isomorphism-invariance ↔ Formality*
B. *Formality → Strong necessity.*

These connections and some of their ramifications are spelled out in theses 1–5 below:

> *Thesis 1: Isomorphism-invariance is formality in the sense of strong structurality.*
>
> *Explanation:* The most distinctive characteristic of properties satisfying the isomorphism-invariance criterion of logicality is their obliviousness to differences between any individuals whatsoever. Isomorphism-invariant properties are blind to such differences. If they hold of anything (in any domain), they hold of everything that can be obtained from it by a 1–1 and onto replacement of actual-counterfactual individuals.
>
> But if isomorphism-invariant properties do not distinguish between any individuals, what do they distinguish between (discern)? Isomorphism-invariant properties discern formal, or strongly structural, patterns of individuals having properties and standing in relations. They distinguish between different formal patterns and between these and nonformal patterns (including arrangements that lack a pattern). For example, *identity* discerns patterns of the type, $\langle \mathbf{a},\mathbf{a} \rangle$, $\langle \mathbf{b},\mathbf{b} \rangle$, ... and it distinguishes between these and any other patterns of pairs of individuals (as well as unpatterned or random pairings); NONEMPTINESS discerns patterns of the type $\langle D,B \rangle$, where B is nonempty (i.e., patterns of the form $\langle D,\{\mathbf{a}, \ldots\} \rangle$), and it distinguishes between these and all other patterns (including $\langle D,\varnothing \rangle$); UNIVERSALITY discerns patterns of the type $\langle D,D \rangle$, and it distinguishes between these and all other patterns (including $\langle D,B \rangle$, where B⊂D); and so on.

The patterns that isomorphism-invariant (maximally invariant) properties distinguish are *strongly*, or *maximally*, structural. They are strongly structural in the sense of not distinguishing between any *isomorphic* structures or patterns. For such properties, all *isomorphic patterns are the same*. Each isomorphism-invariant property identifies a particular strongly structural pattern, and it distinguishes between this pattern and all other patterns (unpatterned collections).[34]

Strong structurality in the sense of invariance-under-all-isomorphisms is naturally viewed as formality. Thus viewed, the isomorphism-invariance criterion is a criterion of *logicality* as *formality*. The characteristic feature of logical properties/constants, according to Thesis 1, is their *formality*.[35]

> *Thesis 2: The formality of logical properties implies the formality of laws governing/describing them.*

Explanation: Take any formal, that is, isomorphism-invariant (maximally invariant) property P. Since P is maximally invariant, it does not distinguish between any two actual-counterfactual individuals. This means that any law/principle that correctly describes P's "behavior" does not distinguish between any actual-counterfactual individuals either. If it did, it would not describe its behavior correctly. The laws governing/describing formal properties are thus formal as well.

> *Thesis 3: The formality of laws/principles governing/describing logical properties implies their necessity; indeed, it implies that theirs is an especially strong type of necessity.*

Explanation: To see how the formality of the laws/principles governing/describing logical properties implies their strong necessity, consider the following two laws/principles:

(8) Every individual is self-identical

or

(8') $(\forall x)x=x$

and

(9) If P is nonempty and every individual that has P has Q, then Q is nonempty

or

---

[34] This conception of strong structurality has points of similarity with mathematical structuralism (Resnik 1981, Shapiro 1997), according to which mathematical individuals are no more than *places in a structure/pattern*.

[35] This kind of formality is objectual, differing from syntactic and technical formality. It coincides with MacFarlane's (2000) second type of formality and has commonalities with his first type as well.

(9') If P is nonempty and is included in Q, then Q is nonempty

or

(9") $[(\exists x)Px \,\&\, (\forall x)(Px \supset Qx)] \supset (\exists x)Qx.$

Since *self-identity,* UNIVERSALITY, NONEMPTINESS, and INCLUSION are invariant under all 1–1 and onto replacements of *actual-counterfactual* individuals, the laws governing/describing them must preserve this trait (Thesis 2). This means, in the case of (8), that *self-identity* is universal among all *actual-counterfactual* individuals in any domain. Consequently, (8) is not just *actually* true but *necessarily* true as well. The same holds for (9). (9) holds in all domains of actual-counterfactual individuals, and as a result, it is necessarily true.

(8) and (9), however, are not simply necessarily true; they are *strongly* necessarily true. To determine the full scope of *maximal* invariance, we have to recognize that not only are maximally invariant properties such as *self-identity* oblivious to differences between any two physically/metaphysically possible individuals, they are oblivious to differences between these and non-physically/metaphysically possible individuals as well (provided they are formally possible). Thus, *self-identity* does not distinguish between a ball that is all-red and small and a ball that is all-red and blue. Being a formal property, *self-identity* is oblivious to color incompatibilities. Although physically/metaphysically, an all-red and blue ball is impossible, *formally* (from a *formal* perspective), it is possible. (Formally, it is just as possible as a ball that is all-red and small.)

This answers a question we posed in the last section: What is the scope of actual-counterfactual individuals in contexts concerning logic? Their scope is very broad. It includes individuals that are physically and even metaphysically impossible. More precisely, it includes all and only *formally possible* individuals. To be formally possible, an individual cannot be formally – hence, logically – contradictory or impossible, but it can be physically or metaphysically contradictory or impossible.[36]

To adequately apply the isomorphism-invariance test of logicality, we have to consider all *formally possible* individuals, including individuals that are physically and metaphysically impossible, such as balls that are both all-red and blue (at the same time). These are the actual-counterfactual individuals that are used

---

[36] The idea of mere formal possibility will seem weird to some readers. It is important to clarify that "formal possibility" is used here as a *theoretical* concept, a *term of art* (not a vernacular concept). As such, it is a powerful and fruitful concept, conducive to an in-depth discussion of logic and mathematics.

both in the logicality (isomorphism-invariance) test and in the construction of models.

So, to correctly identify the invariance of *self-identity*, we consider *all formally possible individuals*. As a result, the counterfactual scope of laws governing *self-identity* is the totality of formal possibilities, which is larger (in the sense of inclusion) than the totality of physical and even metaphysical possibilities. This, in turn, means that the necessity of (8) is extremely high. And the same holds for laws of maximally invariant properties in general. We may say that such laws are *maximally necessary*, and more generally, that laws (correctly) describing *logical* – formal, maximally invariant or isomorphism-invariant – properties have an *especially strong modal force*.

Turning to *LC*, I present the general invariantist solution to the challenges of necessity and formality in two steps: First, in terms of formal laws (Thesis 4), and then in terms of models (Thesis 5). Consider the LC

(10) $(\exists x)(Px \lor Qx), (\forall x) \sim Qx$; therefore, $(\exists x)Px$.

Let us indicate the denotations of the non-*ℓcs* "P" and "Q" by "P" and "Q," and the denotations of the *ℓcs* "$\exists$," "$\lor$," "$\forall$," and "$\sim$" by "NONEMPTY," "$\cup$" (union), "UNIVERSAL" (in an underlying domain), and "‾" (complementation relative to an underlying domain). We can represent the *formal necessity* of (10) by a three-level diagram:

Logic/language	$(\exists x)(Px \lor Qx),$	$(\forall x) \sim Qx$	$\models$	$(\exists x)Px$
			$\updownarrow$	
Truth	$T[(\exists x)(Px \lor Qx)],$	$T[(\forall x) \sim Qx]$	$\Rightarrow$	$T[(\exists x)Px]$
			$\updownarrow$	
World/objects	NONEMPTY$(P \cup Q),$	UNIVERSAL$(\overline{Q})$	➡	NONEMPTY$(P),$

where "$\Rightarrow$" symbolizes formally necessary transmission/preservation of truth, "➡" symbolizes a formal law (objectual formal necessitation), and "$\updownarrow$" stands for "iff." The LC (10) is formally necessary because it is based on a formally necessary objectual law (principle), one that connects the formal pattern delineated by the premises of (10) with the formal pattern delineated by its conclusion. And in general:

> Thesis 4: *LCs are based on objectual laws that are formal (in the invariantist sense) and as such have an especially strong modal force.*

Explanation: Model-theoretically, objectual laws are represented by preservation of truth in all models (for a given language L). Models represent formally possible objectual situations involving formally possible individuals. In greater detail: a model M=<U,δ> consists of a universe of formally possible individuals and a denotation function that assigns to each non-ℓc an individual or a formally possible construct of individuals in U. Each ℓc is assigned a fixed formal denotation in all models. Truth-in-a-model is truth in a formally possible situation. Preservation of truth in all models is based on formal laws, represented by model-theoretic regularities – regularities that hold in all models. Given the large scope of the possibilities represented by models – the totality of formal possibilities (relative to an underlying language L) – preservation of truth in all models represents an especially strong type of necessity: formal necessity. This is captured by:

> *Thesis 5: Consequences satisfying the semantic definition of LC are formally, hence maximally, necessary. Their formal/maximal necessity is due to the fact that they are based on formal-and-necessary laws. These laws connect the formal structures (formal skeletons of the situations) delineated by their premises and conclusions in all models, that is, in all (representations of) formally possible situations (vis-à-vis a given language).*

Conclusion:

Having demonstrated that the formality and necessity requirements are satisfied by the semantic definition of LC for languages with maximally invariant (isomorphism-invariant) ℓcs, we have also demonstrated the adequacy of the general invariantist solution to the logicality challenge.

This solution says that to be logical a constant has to satisfy the formality (maximal-invariance, isomorphism-invariance) criterion of logicality. The adequacy of this criterion depends on whether the consequences it gives rise to satisfy the requirements of necessity and formality. We have now seen that this adequacy condition is satisfied: the formality criterion of logicality, incorporated in the semantic definition of LC, gives rise to consequences that are both formal and necessary (formally necessary).

This concludes our presentation of the integrated solution to the logicality, formality, and necessity challenges. The necessity of LC is due to its formality, which is the basis for the solution to the challenge of logicality. Formality itself is explained in invariantist terms, which play a central role in explaining how it guarantees (an especially strong type of) necessity. This integrated solution is foundational-holistic in the sense of Section 3.2.

We cannot discuss here all the questions that could be, or even have been, asked concerning the semantic definition of LC and the isomorphism-invariance criterion of logicality. But in the next section we will address several questions, and in Sections 6 and 7 we will turn to criticisms.

4 Philosophical Perspective on Logicality and Other Significant Matters

4.1 *Knowledge, Truth, and Logicality*

To further understand the semantic conception of LC and the invariantist approach to logicality, it will be useful to place them in a larger philosophical context. One suitable context is the epistemic context: pursuit of knowledge. Let us begin with what may be called "the basic human cognitive situation." Briefly, we live in a world of which we are a part. For one reason or another, we desire to know and understand this world, not just practically but also theoretically, and not just for instrumental reasons but also for intrinsic reasons – that is, knowledge for its own sake. The knowledge we aim at, however, is not easy to achieve. Our cognitive resources are significantly limited in a variety of ways, and this renders the world highly complex relative to our cognitive capacities. Consequently, knowledge, for us, is not automatic and cannot be taken for granted; we are prone to error and we recognize our fallibility. Nevertheless, we do not give up our epistemic ambitions. We aspire to knowledge of the world *as it is* and *in its full complexity.*

One thing that makes our aspirations at least partially achievable is the circumstance that although we are cognitively limited in significant ways, we also have significant cognitive resources, including both innate and augmented cognitive abilities (sensory perception and intellect, enriched by acquired knowledge) plus the capacity to actively manage our quest for knowledge (by deciding what to investigate, asking questions, designing research programs, building instruments and tools, etc.). All of these make the acquisition of knowledge, at least to some degree, feasible. But the results of our efforts are *always in question.* Given our cognitive limitations (and some of our cognitive endowments – like imagination, which can also lead to error), we face serious obstacles. Consequently, we need tools for determining whether what we, and our theories, say about the world is correct, as well as tools for expanding our knowledge and avoiding pernicious errors. Two such tools are (i) a concept, and a norm, of correctness for our statements and theories – *truth*, and (ii) a universal, effective, and modally strong method of inference that will enable us to move from knowledge we already have to knowledge we do not yet have – *logical inference/consequence.*[37]

Starting with truth: Truth, from this perspective, is a concept, a property, and a norm of correctness for our statements and theories about the world. Given that the pursuit of knowledge, as it is reflected in the basic human cognitive, or cognitive-epistemic, situation, is an attempt to know the *world as it is*, the notion of truth associated with this pursuit is, broadly speaking, a *correspondence* notion. We say that a statement about a given facet of the world is true (has the property of being true) iff what it says holds, in the world, of this facet. The concept of truth denotes this property, and the epistemic norm of truth says that in seeking knowledge of the world we should aim to make statements that possess this property. We may also say that a statement has the property of being true iff it satisfies (or we, in making it, satisfy) the norm of truth.

In saying that from the perspective of the basic human cognitive-epistemic situation truth is correspondence, we must distance ourselves from the naive and overly simplistic characterizations of correspondence as "copy," "picture," "mirror image," or "(direct) isomorphism." The *patterns* of correspondence may be as complex as they need to be (given the complexities of diverse facets of the world on the one hand and our cognitive make-up on the other), and they may vary from one field of knowledge to another. Furthermore, correspondence, as it is conceived in the present context, does not involve either "Kantian noumena" or a "God's eye view." Since, in addition, the methodology we employ is the holistic methodology described in Section 3.2, the present conception of correspondence eschews (at least most of) the common objections, which focus on the naivete of the traditional view, its alleged commitment to a God's eye view, the narrow scope of its correspondence relation, and so on.[38]

Turning to LC: From the present perspective, LC is a tool for expanding our knowledge in light of our cognitive limitations. The question arises: What kind of consequence will fill the bill? The idea of a method for moving from true sentences ("premises") to a true sentence ("conclusion") – from sentences that already belong to our body of knowledge to a sentence that can be added to it in light of its connection to the former – comes to mind. What kind of truth will be transmitted by this method? If our goal is knowledge of the world as it is, and if the concept/norm of truth associated with this goal is a correspondence concept/ norm (broadly conceived), then the appropriate method of consequence has to

---

[37] Such a method could double as a method for weeding pernicious errors, such as contradiction, but I will not discuss this aspect here.

[38] For more on this conception of correspondence, see Sher (2016, chapter 8).

be able to transmit *correspondence truth* (broadly conceived) from premises to conclusion. A powerful method of this kind, based on something that is at work in most fields of knowledge under both actual and counterfactual circumstances, is especially desirable. This leads to the requirements encountered in Section 2: transmission of (correspondence-)truth, formality, and necessity.

How can a method of inference satisfying these requirements be built? If we focus on *formal* properties/operators (in the sense of *maximal-invariance* or *invariance-under-isomorphisms*) and build them into our language as ℓcs, then (as our discussion in Section 3 shows) we can design a method of inference/ consequence that satisfies these requirements. Logical inferences, under this method, will be based on (i) the correlation between ℓcs (language) and formal properties/operators (world); and (ii) laws governing formal properties/operators, which, due to the broad actual-counterfactual scope of the properties/ operators, have an especially strong modal force.

In paradigmatic cases, the method will have three layers: world, truth, and logic. We can represent this schematically by generalizing the diagram given in Section 3.4:

Logic: $\{S_1, S_2, \ldots\} \vDash S$
iff
Truth: $T(S_1), T(S_2), \ldots \Rightarrow T(S)$
iff
World: $\mathfrak{C}_1, \quad \mathfrak{C}_2, \ldots \blacktriangleright \mathfrak{C}.$

In words:

> $S_1, S_2, \ldots$ *logically imply* S
>> iff
>
> the correspondence-truth of $S_1, S_2, \ldots$ *guarantees, with an especially strong modal force*, the correspondence-truth of S
>> iff
>
> the situations, $\mathfrak{C}_1, \mathfrak{C}_2, \ldots$, which do/would make the sentences $S_1, S_2, \ldots$ correspondence-true, and whose formal structures correspond to the logical structures of these sentences, *formally necessitate* the situation $\mathfrak{C}$, which does/would make the sentence S correspondence-true and whose formal structure corresponds to the logical structure of S.

This is a "rational reconstruction" (of a sort) of the semantic method of LC, using any ℓcs denoting formal properties.

Let us conclude with *logicality*. Why is logicality so central to our understanding of LC? In Section 2 we have seen Tarski's demonstration that the issue of logicality is crucial for the proper workings of the semantic definition of LC. But, as we have seen in Section 3, solving the logicality problem does more than that. It enables us to answer deep foundational questions that are difficult to address without it, questions such as "What is LC grounded in?" and "How does/can it transmit truth from premises to conclusions with an especially strong modal force?" The answer, based on the connection between logicality, maximal/isomorphism-invariance, and formality, is that *LC is grounded in formal laws governing the world, laws that due to their formality have an especially strong modal force, and the strong modal force of LC is due to the strong modal force of these laws.* It is because of its fruitfulness in addressing deep foundational questions in a substantive and informative manner that the question of logicality does, and ought to, take a central place in an in-depth study of LC.

4.2 Traditional Features of Logical Consequence

Traditionally, LC has been thought to be general, necessary, formal, topic neutral, certain, normative, analytic, and a priori. On the present analysis, LC is necessary and formal (indeed, necessary in a stronger sense than the traditional, metaphysical, sense and formal in a deeper sense than the merely syntactic traditional sense). Does it also have the other features traditionally attributed to it? Let us start with generality, topic neutrality, and certainty. Here the answer is positive, and the key to this positive answer is the formal necessity of LC.

Generality. If by the generality of LC we understand either truth-preserving in *all* domains of *actual* individuals (to distinguish it from necessity) or applicability in all fields of knowledge, then the generality of consequences satisfying the semantic definition of LC follows from their necessity and formality (maximal invariance).

Topic Neutrality. The topic neutrality of consequences satisfying the semantic definition of LC follows from their formal necessity as well. Consequences satisfying this definition are grounded in laws that have an especially large actual-counterfactual scope and hold regardless of the identity of the individuals and nonlogical/nonformal properties involved. As such, they hold in *all* fields of knowledge, *regardless of their specific topic.*[39] The semantic definition of LC is, thus, topic- (field-, discourse-)neutral.

This is a natural place to correct a common misunderstanding concerning topic neutrality. The topic neutrality of logic is sometimes taken to mean that logic does not have a topic of its own. This is a mistake. Logic does have a topic of its own, namely, logical – formal, necessary, truth-preserving – consequences. But its topic is blind to the topics of other fields, namely, those

---

[39] For the way this includes mathematics, note that all individuals and most properties of standard first-order mathematics are not formal in the present sense.

to which the sentences of different LCs belong. Logic applies to all fields, regardless of *their* topic.

Certainty. Due to their strong invariance, logical properties are indifferent to most facets of reality (to most features of, and differences between, objects). Consequently, the formal laws governing/describing these properties – that is, the laws grounding LCs – are not affected by discoveries concerning most aspects of reality. This means that most new discoveries do not threaten these laws, hence do not threaten our logical judgments. In this sense, logic is highly certain.[40]

What about analyticity and a priority? Historically, many philosophers thought of logic as a priori and analytic. Are consequences satisfying the semantic definition of LC a priori? analytic?

A priority. Traditionally, logic was characterized as purely a priori. Today, however, many philosophers question (on various grounds) the existence of an absolute a priori–empirical bifurcation, replacing the "purely a priori" by the "relative a priori" (Friedman 2001) or "quasi-a priori" (Sher 2016),[41] or treating logic naturalistically (Maddy 2007). The formality cum maximal-invariance of logic suggests that LCs are at least quasi-a priori (or, if we are methodological holists in the sense of Section 3.2, are generally quasi-a priori). Explanation: Due to their strong invariance, LCs are blind to most aspects of reality. This includes, in particular, those aspects of reality that concern nonmaximally invariant properties and are often empirical in the sense of being accessible to sensory perception. Faculties/methods used to study these aspects of reality are not suitable for discovering (establishing) LCs on their own. This is not to say that empirical methods/faculties can play no role at all in the discovery or justification/refutation of claims of LC.[42] But the major burden falls on other faculties/methods.

Analyticity. As a semantic concept (in the Tarskian sense), LC is not analytic. Semantic concepts deal with relations between language and the world, and as such they are not purely linguistic (deal only with meaning). In the case of LC, we have seen that it is significantly grounded in formal

---

[40] It is important to indicate, however, that logic is not certain in other ways: (i) people make mistakes in calculating what follows logically from what all the time; (ii) people, as well theories, can make mistakes concerning what the formal laws are, and these can, and ought to, lead to revisions in logic; (iii) anything concerning LC and its applications, like anything concerning any other subject matter, is open to controversy, disagreement, and revision. Our logical theories, like all other theories, are fallible.

[41] Where, briefly, relative/quasi-a priori knowledge is obtained largely through intellect, but not (necessarily) in complete isolation from experience.

[42] (i) We can use empirical methods to find counterexamples for purported LCs. (ii) Empirical errors can, in principle, be due to formal/logical errors. If, and when, such errors are discovered and their source is correctly identified, they may lead to revision in logic.

laws governing the world, not in purely linguistic principles. Models represent formal possibilities (formally possible ways the world could be or could have been), truth-in-a-model represents truth in a formally possible objectual situation, and preservation of truth in all models is due to objectual regularities of a special kind – namely, formal regularities or laws – that hold in all models/formal-possibilities. Indeed, even the job description of LC – expanding our ability to know the world – suggests that LC is not purely analytic. LC has a linguistic/meaning component, but it also has a (very significant) objectual component.

Finally, normativity. Is LC normative?

4.3 The Normativity of Logical Consequence

The normativity of LC, and of logic more generally, has been the subject of much debate recently. Here I distinguish three questions of normativity: (a) Is there an important sense in which logic is normative, and if there is, what is the source of its normativity? (b) Is the normativity of logic greater than that of other disciplines? (c) Is logic normative in the sense that logical considerations should be put above all other considerations in people's practical decisions? It is the third question that is most closely related to the current debate, but it is the first two that are directly pertinent to the discussion of LC in this Element.

(a) *Is there an important sense in which logic is normative, and if there is, what is the source of its normativity?*

Yes, there is an important sense in which logic is normative, a sense associated with its function or role in the pursuit of knowledge (discussed in Section 4.1). The logical method of consequence is a powerful tool for overcoming at least some of our epistemic limitations. Instead of having to verify each statement directly, by checking its target in the world, logic enables us to affirm the truth of many statements indirectly, based on their connection with other statements that we already know. Our analysis in Sections 2 and 3 showed that, and explained why, the method of LC successfully performs this function, at least in principle, by relying on highly necessary and widely applicable formal laws governing the world. Given the human desire to know the world, this renders logic epistemically normative. Indeed, logic is normative not just for us as pursuers of knowledge, but also for our statements and theories of the world. It is logic's success in performing this epistemic function that is the source of its normativity.

(b) *Is the normativity of logic greater than that of other disciplines?*

There is a sense, due to Frege (1893, 1918), in which all knowledge, and all fields of knowledge, are normative. This is because truth, as such, is normative. Speaking in terms of laws, Frege argued that "[a]ny law asserting what is, can be conceived as prescribing that one ought to think in conformity with it" (1893: 12). The laws of logic, according to Frege, are laws of truth, and consequently, "[f]rom the[se] laws ... there follow prescriptions about asserting, thinking, judging, inferring" (1918: 1).

This may lead us to conclude that all disciplines are equally normative. But our study of LC in this Element enables us to draw distinctions that were not available to Frege. Although truth as a source of normativity places the normativity of logic and that of physics on the same footing, the maximal invariance of logic reveals a sense in which the normativity of logic exceeds that of physics. The strong normativity of consequences satisfying the semantic definition of LC is due to the generality, topic neutrality, necessity, and formality of the laws grounding them. These laws hold for all fields of knowledge, or in other words, all fields of knowledge are bound by these laws. But the opposite is not the case: Logic is not bound by the laws of biology, chemistry, physics, and so on. It disregards, abstracts from, these laws. Chemistry, for example, is not blind to *formal* differences between objects: It distinguishes between a molecule that has EXACTLY-ONE hydrogen atom and a molecule that has EXACTLY-TWO hydrogen atoms, between molecules that have BOTH hydrogen AND oxygen atoms and molecules that have hydrogen BUT NOT oxygen atoms, and so on. Therefore, chemistry, and physics more generally, are subject to the logical laws. However, logic is not subject to their laws. The laws of logic hold for all formally possible objects, regardless of whether they are physically possible or impossible, but the laws of physics do not hold for all logically possible objects. Logic, therefore, is normative for physics (physical laws have to abide by the laws of logic if they are to be true), but physics is not normative for logic. Logic abstracts from the laws of physics, but physics does not abstract from the logical laws. The normativity of logic is thus greater than the normativity of physics, biology, psychology, and other disciplines.

(c) *Is logic normative in the sense that logical considerations should be put above all other considerations in people's practical decisions?*

The debate on the normativity of logic, often traced to Harman (1986), focuses on this question. The question is not whether logic is normative for our theories of the world, that is, whether theories that are logically inconsistent (containing logical contradictions) should be rejected or corrected and whether a given theory T includes, at least in principle, all its LC (i.e., is closed under the relation of LC). The question is whether people, in their everyday life and practical decisions, should put logical considerations above all other considerations, whether they should actually believe (hold in their mind) all the logical consequences of their beliefs, whether they should pay attention to logic always, and in everything they do.

According to Harman, it is not always in the interest of an agent pursuing overall rationality to place the logical norms above all other norms. For example: (1) Just because I believe S_1 and I believe that S_2 follows logically from S_1, does not mean that I am bound to believe S_2. Sometimes it is more rational to stop believing S_1 than to believe S_2. (2) Many LCs of our beliefs are completely useless for us; believing them merely clutters our mind. (3) "Ought" requires a physical-psychological "can," but the logical "ought" does not imply such a "can." (4) It is sometimes rational to have logically incompatible beliefs. Take the particle–wave duality in physics. It may involve logical incompatibility; yet today it is arguably irrational to reject it.

Now, case (1) is sanctioned by logic itself as part of its normativity. Cases (2) and (3) are largely irrelevant to the perspective pursued in this Element. As far as pursuers of knowledge are concerned, we abstract from these concerns, and as far as theories are concerned, these concerns are beside the point. Case (4) is relevant, but it, too, does not conflict with the view that logic is normative. To say that logic is normative for physics, or has greater normativity than physics, is not to say that physicists are bound to avoid logical incompatibilities in all circumstances and at all costs. Harman's conception of normativity is at once too narrow and too strong to account for the normativity of logic from the present perspective. It is too narrow in focusing on single individuals in their day-to-day life. And it is too strong in requiring absolute obedience to norms. The normativity of logic is greater than that of physics in the sense that the logical norms apply to physics but not the other way around. This does not mean, however, that logical considerations always take priority over other considerations. To the extent that there are logical incompatibilities between quantum mechanics and general relativity, they ought to be removed. But given the present state of physical knowledge, physicists may be justified in choosing to relegate the removal of this incompatibility to an open-ended future rather than stopping their physical investigations altogether until they find an acceptable way to remove it.[43]

---

[43] For further discussion of the normativity of logic in response to Harman, see, for example, MacFarlane (2004), "In What Sense (If Any) Is Logic Normative for Thought?" (unpublished manuscript), Field (2009), Steinberger (2019), Russell (2020).

4.4 Is Isomorphism-Invariance a Necessary, Sufficient, or Necessary-and-Sufficient Criterion of Logicality?

The answer to the title question depends on one's conception of the goal of logic. If the goal is to produce consequences that are logical in the sense of being formal, necessary, general, topic neutral, relatively certain, strongly normative, and quasi-a priori, and if we limit our attention to extensional contexts, like those of mathematics, natural science, and parts of other disciplines and everyday discourse, and if we focus on the semantic, model-theoretic aspect of logic and wish to solve the problem of logicality that threatens the Tarskian definition of LC, then, as was shown in Sections 3 and 4.1–4.3, the isomorphism-invariance criterion largely achieves this goal, hence is a necessary-and-sufficient condition of logicality. If the goal is to satisfy additional requirements as well, such as proof-theoretic completeness, simplicity, agreement with the common use of logic in natural language, relevance (in the sense that the content of the premises must be related to the content of the conclusion), and so on, then the criterion is necessary but not sufficient. And if we do not limit our attention to extensional contexts, the criterion is neither necessary nor sufficient.[44] Failure to differentiate these circumstances leads to unnecessary disagreements over the criterion.

4.5 The Scope of Logic; Types of Logic

It is natural to think about the logic that satisfies the invariantist criterion of logicality as a family of logical systems differing in their ℓcs. One member of this family is standard first-order predicate logic, with its familiar ℓcs. Many philosophers view this as the *terra firma* of logic. But, as we have seen in Sections 3 and 4.1–4.4, any variant of standard first-order logic with a collection of ℓcs sanctioned by the isomorphism-invariance criterion yields LCs that are just as formal, necessary, general, topic neutral, relatively certain, strongly normative, and quasi-a priori (in the sense explained earlier) as those of standard first-order logic. In the literature, nonstandard members of the family of first-order logics satisfying the invariance-under-isomorphism criterion are called "generalized logics," "abstract logics," "model-theoretic logics," and so on, and the nonstandard quantifiers of these logics are called "generalized quantifiers."

---

[44] For a relevant discussion of nonextensionality (intensionality), see, for example, Fitting (2015).

Scope of Logic Thesis (Mostowski 1957, Barwise 1985, Sher 1991)

> *Standard first-order logic does not exhaust the totality of (mathematical, predicate) logical systems. These systems include generalized first-order logics, (full) second-order logic, and other logics with ℓcs satisfying the isomorphism-invariance criterion.*

Clearly, not every genuine logical system based on this thesis is of interest to philosophers and logicians. This is a normal situation. Just as not all sets are of interest to set theorists and not all numbers are of interest to number theorists, so not all logical properties/constants, and not all logical systems containing such properties/constants, are of interest to philosophers and logicians. But some are. Most importantly: A general principle of logicality is of considerable theoretic interest for both philosophers and logicians.

We can also characterize the scope of logics satisfying the invariance-under-isomorphism criterion in terms of the totality of properties satisfying this criterion (admissible denotations of ℓcs). Here we have the following interesting result:

Scope of Logical Properties

> *All higher-level correlates of first-level mathematical properties are invariant under isomorphisms (although most first-level mathematical properties are not)*[45] *(Lindström 1966, Tarski 1966/1986, Sher 1991, McGee 1996).*

We will discuss the relation between logic and mathematics in the next section.

I have noted that the logics satisfying the isomorphism-invariance criterion of logicality are intended for use in extensional contexts. This does not mean that they have no role to play in intensional contexts, such as propositional-attitude contexts. Consider the propositional-attitude context of belief. Let B be a belief operator and "Ba(S)" mean "a believes that S," where S is a sentence. First, extensional LCs hold outside the scope of the belief operator. For example: "$(\forall x)Bx(S)$; therefore, Ba(S)" is a genuine LC. Second, under certain conditions, extensional LCs may be adjusted so that they hold within the scope of the belief operator . For example, while "Ba(S$_1$), S$_1 \supset$ S$_2$; therefore, Ba(S$_2$)" is not a genuine LC, under certain conceptions of belief it can be adjusted (e.g., by replacing "S$_1 \supset$ S$_2$" with "Ba(S$_1 \supset$ S$_2$)") so that the result is a genuine LC.

An example of a logic that includes fixed ("distinguished") constants/operators that do not satisfy the isomorphism-invariance criterion is *modal logic*. In modal logic, we add one or two modal operators, the necessity and/or possibility sentential operators, which are not isomorphism-invariant, to standard first-order logic (or indeed to any predicate logic with ℓcs satisfying the invariantist

---

[45] For example, the first-level mathematical properties *is-1* ($x=1$), *is-even*, and *is-a-member-of* ($\in$) are not isomorphism-invariant.

criterion). By further expanding the Tarskian semantic apparatus (e.g., adding so-called possible worlds), we expand the domain of consequences studied by logic.

For an example of contracting the range of consequences studied by logic, take *relevance logic*. By requiring that the content of the premises be relevant to the content of the conclusion it pronounces, the otherwise logically valid consequence "Snow is white and snow is not white; therefore, whales are mammals" nonlogically valid. These logical systems raise the idea of logical pluralism. We will comment on this idea in the next section.

4.6 Background Theory, Bivalence, Logic, and Mathematics

(a) *Formal Laws and Background Theory of Formal Structure*

LC, semantically defined as above, is grounded in formal laws. Models represent the totality of formal possibilities and preservation of truth in all models is grounded in laws governing all formal possibilities. But how do we determine *what* the formal laws are? Both the semantic definition of LC and the invariantist criterion of logicality are couched in some background theory, and it is this theory that tells us what the formal laws are (what the totality of models is and what laws govern this totality). In current practice, as we have noted, the background theory is standard first-order set theory, usually ZFC; in Tarski's 1936 (1983 [1936a]) and 1966/1986 papers, the background theory was Russellian theory of types.

> Question (1) Is it inherent in the semantic definition of LC and the invariantist criterion of logicality that they are couched either in ZFC or in the theory of types?

Clearly, the answer to this question is negative. To be implemented in a precise manner, the general, largely philosophical, ideas guiding the definition of LC and the criterion of logicality require an appropriate precisification. Such a precisification, in turn, requires the tools of an appropriate background theory. But it does not inherently require a particular background theory. What we have learned so far is that an appropriate background theory must be, or include, a theory of *formal structure*, but not that it must be, or include, ZFC or the theory of types. While it seems natural to view these two theories as theories of formal structure, ultimately, it is an open question whether they are optimal, or even adequate, for the task.

It is important to recognize that in principle, the ideas expressed by the semantic definition of LC and the associated criterion of logicality are compatible with multiple precisifications using diverse background theories. In fact, it is generally prudent not to overprecisify, because readers' prior bias against a given precisification may turn them against a general philosophical idea that is not dependent on this particular precisification and can in principle be precisified in other ways. (I will return to this point in Section 5.2.) The definitions of LC and logicality require an appropriate background theory, but the choice of a background theory is a metatask, one that goes beyond the definitions themselves.

> Question (2) Is it inherent in the semantic definition of LC that it is grounded in particular formal laws and not others?

The answer is "yes in one way, no in another." To be adequate, the semantic definition of LC must be grounded in formal laws that in fact govern (correctly describe) the world. But it is an open question what these laws are. As in any other field, we have to rely on what we think are the true formal laws, while keeping an open mind and exercising critical attitude toward our current beliefs.

(b) *Bivalence*

Following, for example, Dummett (1978), bivalence is naturally thought to be inherent in the correspondence conception of truth and the "classical" approach to logic, which is often associated with the Tarskian definition of LC. But the present study suggests that neither is the case. The question of bivalence has to do with the formal structure of the world (the formal behavior of properties in the world). Let me explain. Given a domain D, every 1-place first-level (extensional) property P divides it into subdomains. If the formal structure of the world is bivalent, every property divides it into two disjoint subdomains: the collection of all P's in D and the collection of all non-P's in D. The former is included in D; the latter is its *complement* in D. Given an individual in D, there are exactly two possibilities: either it has P or it does not. If this is not the case, the world is not bivalent. If (extensional) properties divide an arbitrary D to, say, three subdomains, the world is trivalent. This extends to n-place first-level properties. Now, it is an open question whether the world is bivalent (whether properties divide a given domain into two or more subdomains). And both the possibility that the world is (formally) bivalent and the possibility that it is (formally) nonbivalent are compatible with the correspondence conception of truth as well with the general principles underlying the semantic definition of LC. The common background theory of logic, ZFC, is bivalent. But, as we have noted, it is an open question, one that goes beyond the semantic definition of LC, whether it gets the formal structure of the world (the formal behavior of properties) right. Whether logic is bivalent, then, depends on the formal structure of the world (as expressed by the totality of formal possibilities and formal laws).

In this context, it is important to note that trivalent properties, just like bivalent properties, can be *formal* in the sense of being maximally invariant, where maximal-invariance is precisified in a way that is compatible with trivalence.

This leads to a note on *pluralism*. Logical pluralism is the view that there is, in principle, more than one "good" logic. This view has been advocated on several grounds. From the present perspective we divide logical pluralism to three positions: (1) There is no question of truth or correctness in logic, only a question of convenience. (2) There is a question of truth in logic, but there are incompatible true logics. (3) The development of new logics is a worthwhile enterprise, encouraging innovation and potentially leading to new discoveries. The investigations in this Element are compatible with (3) but incompatible with (1). As for (2), we need to distinguish between genuine and nongenuine conflicts. Interest in diverse contexts, as well as variations in perspectives and goals, understandably lead to multiple logics that do not conflict with each other, for example, mathematical logic, modal logic, and relevance logic. It is also possible in principle that different parts of the world (e.g., its macroscopic and microscopic parts) differ in their formal structure, hence require different logics. But given the same context, the same perspective, the same interests, and a formally uniform world, conflicting logics cannot all be correct. The values cherished by logical pluralists – charity, generosity, "let a thousand flowers bloom" – are humanistic values that have their correlates in the general epistemic sphere: open-mindedness, willingness to experiment, broad perspective, nondogmatic evaluation of new theories, and so on. But truth, critical justification, and taking epistemic responsibility for our theories are also deeply humanistic values. Logic, like any other field of knowledge, is subject to veridicality constraints, and one should always be careful not to confuse tolerance toward new ideas with tolerance toward error. Pluralism of type (2) can easily slide into type (1) pluralism.

(c) *Relation between logic and mathematics*

In the logical and philosophical literature we find two dominant views: (1) logic and mathematics are the same discipline; (2) logic and mathematics are separate disciplines. The most well-known representative of (1) is the logicist program, which claims that mathematics is reducible to logic, and whose main representatives are Frege (1967 [1879], 1893) and Russell (Whitehead and Russell 1910–1913/1925–1927, Russell 1971 [1919]). The main advocates of (2) are W. V. Quine (1970/1986) on the one hand and contemporary mathematicians such as Feferman (see Section 6.1) on the other. Where do the semantic definition of LC and the related criterion of logicality stand on this issue?

The semantic definition of LC, by itself, appears to be agnostic with respect to this question. The isomorphism-invariance criterion of logicality has more to say. First, it implies that mathematics and logic are not identical and neither is assimilated to the other. This follows from the result, reported in Section 4.5, that most first-level mathematical properties are not logical. But while first-level mathematical properties are not strictly speaking logical, they *are correlated* with higher-level mathematical properties, which *are* logical. Is this correlation significant? Two different answers to this question are given by Tarski (1966/1986) and Sher (1991, 2016):

(i) Tarski's answer is that it is not: we can view logic and mathematics as assimilated to each other or as separate from each other, as we please. Philosophers, who like unity, are likely to prefer the first view; mathematicians, "on the other hand, would be disappointed to hear that mathematics, which they consider the highest discipline in the world, is a part of something so trivial as logic" (1966/1986: 153).

(ii) Sher's answer (1991, 2016) is that it is. Logic and mathematics have a common core, which is *the formal*. But neither is fully assimilated (or reducible) to the other. There is a *division of labor* between them: Mathematics studies the formal, logic uses it to build a powerful system of inference. At the same time, the two disciplines are interconnected: Mathematics uses logic as a framework for formulating mathematical theories while logic uses mathematics as a background theory of formal structure. Methodologically, logic and mathematics develop in tandem, in a back-and-forth (Neurathian) process. Starting from some basic logic-mathematics (say, Boolean algebra), we construct a simple logic and simple mathematical theories (say, sentential/syllogistic logic and naive set theory). These are used to construct a more sophisticated logic (say, standard first-order predicate logic), which is used to construct more sophisticated mathematical theories (say, axiomatic set theory). These give rise to new, still more sophisticated, logics (e.g., generalized logics), and so on.[46]

What is the significance of the fact that higher-level mathematics is formal in the invariance sense, but lower-level mathematics is not? This fact can be interpreted in a number of ways. One of these leads to a novel view of mathematics (with some roots in Frege). Mathematics as a whole is, or studies, the formal, which is for the most part higher-level. But humans' cognitive make-up favors dealing with first-level rather than higher-level structures. To accommodate

---

[46] The talk about the joint development of logic and mathematics here is intended in the sense of a Carnapian-like rational reconstruction. One can also view it as a genetic, or an in-principle, account.

this, humans study higher-level formal properties by studying their lower-level (nonformal) correlates. They posit zero-level mathematical entities, such as numbers or sets (conceived as individuals), to represent second-level formal properties such as cardinalities. For example, the numerical individual 1 represents the second-level cardinality property EXACTLY-ONE, and so on. (For further discussion, see Sher 2016, section 8.4.)

(d) *Metaphysics and Logic*

Are *formal* necessity and possibility the same things as *metaphysical* necessity and possibility? Strictly speaking, it is difficult to answer this question due to the heterogeneity of metaphysics. On the one hand, metaphysics deals with extremely broad and basic issues, such as objects or the world in the broadest sense of the word. On the other hand, it deals with narrower and more specific issues such as causality, free will, and perhaps color incompatibilities (the impossibility of an object being both all-red and blue).[47] Accordingly, it is not even clear whether there is *unique* scope of *metaphysical* necessity/possibility. But clearly, in terms of invariance, formal possibility is broader than the narrower types of physical possibility.

4.7 Salient Metalogical Theorems

There are many salient metalogical results concerning the semantic definition of LC and the isomorphism-invariance criterion of logicality. The former (with proofs) can be found in most standard textbooks of mathematical logic; the latter in various collections and journal articles. Here I limit myself to a small sample of results that are directly relevant to this Element (without proofs).

First, let me note that the semantic definition of LC immediately leads to semantic definitions of other metalogical concepts:

Semantic Definitions of Metalogical Concepts

> *Logical truth:* S is logically true iff S is true in all models.
> *Logical falsehood:* S is logically false iff S is false in all models.
> *Logical indeterminacy:* S is logically indeterminate iff S is true in some models and false in others.
> *Logical equivalence:* S_1 and S_2 are logically equivalent iff they have the same truth value in all models.
> *Logical consistency:* Γ is logically consistent iff it has at least one model.

---

[47] It was this type of possibility that I had in mind when I said earlier that formal possibility is broader than metaphysical possibility.

Second, important metalogical results are illuminatingly expressed in terms of LC or models.

Examples:[48]

Completeness of Standard First-order Logic (SFOL) (Gödel 1986 [1929])

$\Gamma \vdash_{SFOL} S$ *iff* $\Gamma \vDash_{SFOL} S$.[49]

Incompleteness of Full Second-order Logic (FSOL) (Gödel 1986 [1931])[50]

NOT [$\Gamma \vdash_{FSOL} S$ iff $\Gamma \vDash_{FSOL} S$].

Compactness of Standard First-order Logic (Gödel 1986 [1929])

Γ *has a model iff every finite subset of* Γ *has a model.*

Löwenheim–Skolem–Tarski Theorem for Standard First-order Logic (Löwenheim 1967 [1915], Skolem 1967 [1920], Tarski and Vaught 1957)

Γ *has an infinite model iff for every infinite cardinal* κ, Γ *has a model with a universe of cardinality* κ.

The downward Löwenheim–Skolem theorem says that if Γ has a model of any infinite cardinality κ, then Γ has a model of cardinality $\aleph_0$ (the smallest infinite cardinality).

Third, there are interesting results concerning the isomorphism-invariance criterion of logicality.

Examples:

Lindström's Theorem (1969)

Standard first-order logic is the strongest first-order logic in which both the compactness theorem and the downward Löwenheim–Skolem theorem hold.

Keisler's Theorem (1970)

First-order logic with the quantifier "there-exist-uncountably-many" is complete.

These theorems are too rich for a comprehensive discussion in this Element, but a few brief points may be useful.

(a) *The Completeness and Incompleteness Theorems.*

　　(i) In its current formulation, the completeness theorem is naturally under-stood as stating the coextensionality of the proof-theoretic and semantic concepts of LC in standard first-order logic. In the past it was often understood as stating the completeness of the proof- (or axiomatic-)

---

[48] Assuming both the underlying language and Γ are countable.

[49] Completeness is sometimes divided into two parts: soundness and completeness proper. A logical system is sound iff for every Γ and S, if $\Gamma \vdash S$, then $\Gamma \vDash S$; it is (properly) complete iff for every Γ and S, if $\Gamma \vDash S$, then $\Gamma \vdash S$. Soundness is commonly considered a necessary requirement on an acceptable logical system; (proper) completeness is not.

[50] Full second-order logic is standard second-order logic in which the second-order variables range over all subsets of the universe in any model.

system of standard first-order logic (relative to an informal conception of LC in terms of truth).

(ii) Gödel's incompleteness theorem is usually formulated as a meta*mathematical* theorem saying that there is no complete axiomatization A of any reasonably strong mathematical theory T (e.g., Peano Arithmetic), assuming it is logically consistent. That is, given such a T, there is no axiomatization A of T such that all the true sentences of T are provable in A. Here the theorem is formulated as a meta*logical* theorem concerning higher-order logics. (Since FSOL is sufficiently strong to formulate all of mathematics – all mathematical truths follow logically from the axioms of FSOL – this logic is incomplete in the metalogical sense.)

(b) *The Completeness Theorem and Keisler's Theorem.* Following Quine (1970/1986), many philosophers and logicians consider completeness a necessary condition for an adequate logic. Furthermore, assuming that standard first-order logic is the strongest complete logic, some philosophers/logicians argue that *logic = standard first-order logic* and all stronger predicate/mathematical logics are not genuine logics (see Section 6.1). But their assumption is incorrect. Theorems such as Keisler's show that some stronger logics (ones that properly include standard first-order logic) are complete.

(c) *The Completeness, Compactness, Downward Löwenheim–Skolem, and Lindström Theorems.* In light of these theorems, the question arises whether the completeness, compactness, and the downward Löwenheim–Skolem properties[51] are intrinsic, or mandatory, for logical systems. While having these properties simplifies logical systems and increases their efficiency (it is far easier to deal with finite sets of sentences and countable models than with infinite sets of sentences or uncountable models), philosophically, the answer appears to be negative. Barwise expressed this by saying that to require logic to have these properties is to "confuse ... [its] subject matter ... with ... its tools" (Barwise 1985: 6). Compactness, for example, is a useful tool, but it does not capture the subject matter of logic. And in general, the fact that some logical systems are easier to work with than others does not mean that the latter are not genuinely logical. For example, sentential logic, being weaker than predicate logic, has features (e.g., decidability) that make it easier to work with than the latter. But this does not justify rejecting predicate logic as nonlogical. The same holds for weak predicate logics. Being relatively weak, standard first-order logic has features that are not found in stronger logics. But this does not render the

---

[51] That is, the properties of being a complete logical system, a compact logical system, and so on.

latter nonlogical. On the contrary, stronger logics have greater expressive power and as such can identify LCs that standard first-order logic cannot identify. To the extent that the idea of logicality as formality (in the sense explained in Section 3 and further discussed in the present section) explains the subject matter of logic, all formal logics are genuine logics.

4.8 Confusions Concerning Tarski's 1966/1986 Paper

Tarski's 1966/1986 paper led to confusions concerning the *criterion of logicality* advanced by the so-called Tarski–Sher thesis. We have already addressed one of these confusions, concerning invariance under permutations (see Section 3.3).

A second confusion concerns *generality*. Whereas Tarski (1983 [1936a]) introduced formality and necessity as the distinctive characteristics of LC, his 1966/1986 paper introduced generality as the distinctive characteristic of logicality. This is not surprising in light of the fact that Tarski's later paper completely disregarded his earlier one, being focused on Klein's Erlangen Program, where differences in generality between various geometries play a significant role, expressed in invariantist terms. Tarski's invariantist project extended Klein's focus on generality to logic:

> Now suppose we continue this idea, and consider still wider classes of transformations. In the extreme case, we would consider the class of *all* one-one transformations of the space, or universe of discourse, or "world," onto itself. What will be the science which deals with the notions invariant under this widest class of transformations? Here we will have very few notions, all of a very general character. I suggest that they are the logical notions, that we call a notion "logical" if it is invariant under all possible one-one transformations of the world onto itself. (Tarski 1966/1986: 149)

Readers who arrive at the Tarski–Sher thesis through Tarski (1966/1986) tend to identify logicality with utmost generality. But this is problematic.[52] As explained by Bonnay (2008), invariance under all isomorphisms does not represent maximal generality. Such invariance is invariance under functions of a special kind: 1–1 and onto. Invariance under functions of a more general kind would yield more general notions. In the extreme case, properties that are invariant under all functions of any kind would be far more general. The problem is that they would be too general. None of the standard ℓcs (perhaps with the exception of identity) are invariant under all functions. The properties of utmost generality (in the invariance sense) are, for

---

[52] It is not clear to me whether Tarski himself intended "generality" in the sense discussed in what follows. However, in principle, it is important to understand the sense in which logicality is not utmost generality.

the most part, semantic-type notions, such as "is-an-individual," "is-a-first-level-1-place-property," and so on. Logics whose ℓcs are limited to these notions are too impoverished to fulfill the task of logic (see Sections 2–3 and 4.1–4.7) or, indeed, to resemble anything regarded as logic at the present or in the past. In particular, a criterion that identifies logicality with utmost generality would not classify even most of the standard first-order ℓcs as logical, and as such would severely undergenerate.

The Sher side of the Tarski–Sher thesis identifies logicality with formality rather than with utmost generality. This enables the thesis to classify all the standard ℓcs as logical as well as to ensure satisfaction of the adequacy condition of formality (for a definition of LC). This also ensures considerable generality, as we have seen, though not maximal generality. On this conception, it is formality, rather than generality, that is the distinctive characteristic of the isomorphism-invariance criterion and the properties/constants satisfying it.

Another confusion arises from Tarski's statement that "it turns out that our logic ... is a logic of number, of numerical relations" (Tarski 1966/1986: 151). This led some philosophers to view the isomorphism-invariance criterion of logicality as identifying logicality with a very narrow aspect of formality, namely, *number* (cardinality, quantity). However, if we examine the criterion itself, we see that this is not the case. While cardinality properties are isomorphism-invariant, so are many other formal properties – IS-SYMMETRIC, IS-REFLEXIVE, IS-TRANSITIVE, IS-AN-ORDERING-RELATION, IS-A-WELL-ORDERING-RELATION, IS-AN-EQUIVALENCE-RELATION, and so on – which have nothing to do with numbers. There is no question that Tarski recognized this fact. Indeed, this citation about numbers was given in the context of a discussion of the most basic type of second-level logical properties: 1-place second-level properties of 1-place first-level properties. Following the discussion of this basic type, Tarski said:

> If you turn to more complicated notions, for instance to relations between [properties], then the variety of logical notions increases. Here for the first time you come across many important and interesting logical relations, well known to those who have studied the elements of logic. I mean such things as inclusion between [properties], disjointness of two [properties], overlapping of two [properties], and many others; all these are examples of logical relations in the normal sense, and they are also logical in the sense of my suggestion. (Tarski 1966/1986: 151)

Logic, according to the isomorphism-invariance criterion, centers on formal properties in general, not specifically on numerical properties.

In the next two sections we turn to criticisms of the semantic definition of LC and the isomorphism-invariance criterion of logicality.

5 Criticisms of the Semantic Definition of Logical Consequence

Both the semantic definition of LC and the isomorphism-invariance criterion of logicality have been subject to criticisms. In examining these criticisms, it is especially important to pay attention to incongruities between the ideas that actually belong to the definition/criterion in question and the ideas attributed to them by the critics. Only when the two are congruent are the criticisms genuine. In this section I discuss criticisms of the semantic definition of LC, in the next section, criticisms of the isomorphism-invariance criterion of logicality.

5.1 The Representational and Interpretational Duality

In his 1990 book on LC, Etchemendy stated that:

> Tarski's analysis [of LC] is wrong, ... his account ... does not capture, or
> even come close to capturing, any pretheoretic conception of [this] logical
> propert[y]. (Etchemendy 1990: 6)

His criticism did not end with Tarski:

> [T]he standard, semantic account of logical consequence is mistaken. ...
> [W]hen we apply the account to arbitrary languages ... it will regularly and
> predictably define a relation at variance with the genuine consequence rela-
> tion for the language in question. The definition will both *undergenerate* and
> *overgenerate*: it will declare certain arguments invalid that are actually valid,
> and declare others valid that in fact are not. (Etchemendy 1990: 8)

Etchemendy made two claims, one historical, the other not. The historical claim is that in his 1936 paper (1983 [1936a]), Tarski provided an incorrect justification of the claim that his semantic definition of LC satisfies the adequacy condition of necessity (see Section 2.3); in fact, it fails to satisfy this condition. The other claim is that the contemporary version of this defin-ition fails as well, and indeed is bound to fail.

Concerning the historical criticism, Tarski claimed that his definition's satis-faction of the necessity condition *could be proven*. Etchemendy attributed to Tarski a faulty proof of this claim, involving an elementary error in handling modal operators. This alleged error Etchemendy called "*Tarski's Fallacy*" (Etchemendy 1990: 85). The fallacy consists in proving

(11) **Nec** $[\Gamma \vDash S \supset [T(\Gamma) \supset T(S)]]$

instead of

(12) $\Gamma \vDash S \supset$ **Nec** $[T(\Gamma) \supset T(S)]$.

This is a fallacy since (11) does not imply (12).[53]

As we have seen in Section 2.6, however, Tarski never spelled out the proof he had in mind or even hinted at what it might be. Etchemendy provided no evidence for attributing to Tarski the fallacious proof. In the absence of such evidence, the criticism is a strawman.

Turning to Etchemendy's more general claim, it is based on analysis of the options available for a model-theoretic definition of LC. Etchemendy assumed there were two such options, so-called representational and interpretational. He claimed that neither is adequate, and concluded that the semantic definition fails.

To understand Etchemendy's argument, we need to understand what is meant by "representational" and "interpretational". Etchemendy distinguished between two types of model-theoretic semantics, according to what models represent. He assumed there are two relevant parameters: world and language (interpretation of linguistic expressions). What models represent is determined by which parameter changes from model to model.

Representational Semantics (Etchemendy 1990: 20–21)
  1. The world varies from model to model; language is held fixed in all models.
  2. Models represent ways our world could be (could have been).

  Elaboration: What is held fixed in all models is the meaning or interpretation of linguistic expressions. What changes is the way the world is. Models represent possible worlds in the intuitive or metaphysical sense.

Interpretational Semantics (Etchemendy 1990: 56–61)
  1. Language varies from model to model; the world is fixed.
  2. Models represent ways our language could be (could have been).

  Elaboration: What is held fixed in all models is the actual world. What varies is the interpretation/denotation of the non-ℓcs of the language in the actual world. The difference between logical and non-ℓcs is simply a difference between constants whose interpretation is held fixed in all models and constants whose interpretation changes from model to model. Which constants are fixed/changing is unprincipled or arbitrary.

Both representational and interpretational semantics succeed in capturing the intuitive notion of LC in some cases. For example, when they assume the standard division of constants into logical and nonlogical, both identify the following consequence as logical:

---

[53] In general, this fallacy is that of confusing "**Nec**$(S_1 \supset S_2)$" with "$S_1 \supset$**Nec**(S_2)." To see that the former does not imply the latter, consider the case of $S_1 = S_2$.

(3) Tarski is a logician; therefore, something is a logician.

In Symbols:

(3") L*t*; therefore, (∃x)Lx

Representational semantics identifies (3) as logical based on the fact that no matter how the actual world is or could have been, if the property *is-a-logician* holds of Tarski in it, it is nonempty in it. In other words: (∀ possible-world M)[T_M(Lt)⊃T_M((∃x)Lx)]. Interpretational semantics identifies (3) as logical based on the fact that no matter what the nonfixed constants "logician" and "Tarski" mean or denote in the actual world, if the actual individual denoted by "Tarski" (whatever it is) has the property denoted by "logician" (whatever it is) in the actual world, then this property is nonempty in the actual world. In other words: (∀ possible-interpretation-of-the-language-in-the-actual-world M) [T_M(Lt) ⊃ T_M((∃x)Lx)].

Assuming the standard demarcation of non-ℓcs, both also identify the following consequence as nonlogical:

(1) Tarski is a logician; therefore, Frege is a logician.

In symbols:

(1") L*t*; therefore, L*f*.

Representational semantics does this based on the fact that the world could have been such that Tarski is a logician but Frege is not. Some models represent this possibility, and in it (1) is not truth-preserving. Interpretational semantics shows this based on the fact that "logician" could have meant "Polish" in the given language (while "Tarski" and "Frege" retained their usual meaning/denotation). (1) is not truth-preserving in a model that represents this possibility.

In spite of capturing the intended concept of LC in some cases, however, both the representational and the interpretational versions of the semantic definition of LC are, in the end, inadequate.

Concerning the representational version, Etchemendy argued that the intuitive/metaphysical conception of possible worlds is too vague, obscure, and indeterminate to be rendered precise by a mathematical apparatus of models:

> It is ... clear that representational semantics affords no net increase in the precision or mathematical tractability of [the] notion [of LC]. Any obscurity attaching to the bare concept of necessary truth will reemerge when ... we ask whether our models represent all and only genuinely possible configurations of the world. (Etchemendy 1990: 25)

Etchemendy concluded that a successful definition of LC cannot be representational. Assuming the dilemma "the semantic definition of LC is either representational or interpretational," he further concluded that the semantic definition of LC is interpretational. But the interpretational definition, he pointed out, fails. Consider the consequence:

(2) There is exactly one individual; therefore, There are at least two individuals.

In symbols (assuming the standard division of constants into logical and non-logical):

(2') $(\exists x)(\forall y)x=y$; therefore, $(\exists x)(\exists y)x \neq y$.

Clearly, (2) is not a genuine LC. But due to the facts that (i) all the constants of (2) are logical, hence their interpretation is fixed in all models, and (ii) in interpretational semantics all models have the same universe, namely, the actual universe, which has more than one individual, the premise of (2) is false in all models (/its conclusion is true in all models), hence it is truth-preserving in all models.[54]

Assuming the above dilemma, Etchemendy concluded that the semantic definition of LC fails.

Responses. Many philosophers – McGee (1992a, 1992b), García-Carpintero (1993), Jacquette (1994), Schurz (1994), Priest (1995), Gómez-Torrente (1996), Ray (1996), Sher (1996), Chihara (1998), S. Shapiro (1998) – criticized Etchemendy's claims (e.g., that the semantic definition of LC is interpretational, that it is either interpretational or representational [in Etchemendy's sense], that it fails to satisfy the adequacy condition of necessity, that it reduces LC to MC, that universes of models are limited to actual individuals), as well as Etchemendy's neglect of the formality condition (which is a key to understanding how necessity is obtained), his failure to distinguish *epistemic* and *definitional* adequacy, and so on.[55]

Evaluation. In evaluating Etchemendy's criticisms, I will focus on their congruity/incongruity with the actual definition of LC and its guiding ideas. Points of congruity include (i) two central parameters of semantic definitions are *language* and *world*; and (ii) an adequate definition of LC must satisfy the condition of *necessity*. Points of incongruity include: (i) neglect of the adequacy condition of formality; (ii) failure to appreciate the logicality (ℓcs) challenge; and (iii) false interpretational-or-representational dilemma.

---

[54] If, as in Etchemendy (2008), interpretational models are allowed to represent nonempty subsets of the universe of the actual world, replace (2) by "There are at least n+1 individuals; therefore, there are at least n+2 individuals," where n is the number of individuals in the actual world.

[55] For Etchemendy's response to these criticisms see Etchemendy (2008).

Elaboration. In principle, there are multiple ways in which *language* and *world* can be integrated into the model-theoretic apparatus. Etchemendy considers only one possibility: One of these parameters is fixed, the other varies from model to model. This leaves exactly two options: Either language is fixed and the world varies (representational option), or the world is fixed and language varies (interpretational option). But in fact, both language and world are *partly* fixed, *partly* variable in the semantic apparatus of LC. The fixed elements are the *ℓcs* (language) and their formal denotations (world), as well as the formal laws/principles governing models (world). The variable elements are the non-*ℓcs* (language) and their denotations (world), as well the universes of models (world) and the nonformal properties of objects.

This means that logical models are neither interpretational nor representational (in Etchemendy's sense). They are not interpretational because language is partly fixed (*ℓcs* are) and the world is partly variable (universes and nonformal features of objects vary); they are not representational because language is partly variable (non-*ℓcs*) and the world is partly fixed (formal laws/principles governing models are). In addition, models represent *formal* possibilities, not intuitive/metaphysical possibilities.

Etchemendy's inattention to the (semantic) *formality* of LC (which implies its necessity) and his claim that the semantic definition is interpretational lead him to incorrectly say that regularities that hold in all models are merely contingent and that the problem of *ℓcs* is a "red herring"[56] (Etchemendy 1990: 129).

5.2 Set-theoretic Models

The semantic definition of LC has been criticized not just for its alleged failure to yield necessary consequences – consequences that necessarily preserve truth from premises to conclusion – but even for its alleged failure to yield MCs – consequences that preserve truth simpliciter, that is, preserve truth in the actual world. Thus, Field said:

> [W]e must reject the claim that all logically valid inferences preserve truth. (Field 2009: 263)

This criticism is directed specifically at the current definition of models, which is given in first-order set-theoretic terms, and it is especially clear when

---

[56] Since solving it would not make the interpretational definition right.

L itself is the language of standard first-order set theory. In this language, sets are denoted by individual terms, that is, sets are construed as individuals. Now, the reality (world) of sets includes *proper-class*-many sets, but models are limited to universes with *proper-set*-many individuals.[57] Hence, the actual world of sets is not represented by any model. That is to say:

> [C]lassical models misrepresent reality: classical models have domains restricted in size whereas set-theoretic reality doesn't. (Field 2009: 264–265)

In greater detail, McGee said:

> The ... problem ... turns upon the richness of the mathematical universe ... [T]he question [is] whether the universe of set theory is robust enough so that we can find within it a model of each aspect of the actual world. The domain of a model is always a set, and there is no set which includes everything, so there is no model which comprehends the world as a whole. Rather, each model represents only a part of the world. That being the case, how can we be so sure that, if a sentence [S] is false, there is some model in which [S] is false? Perhaps the falsity of [S] depends upon some feature of the world as a whole which isn't reflected in any model. Until we can rule out this possibility, we cannot be assured that a sentence true in every model is also true. (McGee 1992b: 278)

The criticism that LC, semantically defined, fails to preserve truth (simpliciter) immediately leads to the further criticism that it fails to satisfy the necessity requirement. If LC does not preserve truth, it does not preserve truth necessarily. This leads to the negative conclusion:

> [L]ogic *can't* be the science of what forms of inference necessarily preserve truth – even if the necessity in question is restricted to ... *necessity by virtue of logical form.* (Field 2009: 252)

McGee (2004) illustrated the problem using a generalized quantifier, $\exists^{AI}$, which denotes the property THERE-ARE-ABSOLUTELY-INFINITELY-MANY (THERE-ARE-PROPER-CLASS-MANY). Consider the sentence "$(\exists^{AI}x)x=x$," which says that there are proper-class-many things. This sentence is true (there are proper-class-many sets), hence is not logically false. But it is false in all set-theoretic models, since no model has proper-class-many individuals. Hence, it is logically false according to the semantic definition of LC/truth.

Both McGee and Field emphasized that this problem is limited to a very narrow array of cases, saying that the semantic definition is perfectly

---

[57] In standard set theory, the collection of all sets is not a set (to avoid paradox). It is too large to be a set. It is a *proper class*. (Every set is a class but not every class is a set. A set that is not a class is a *proper set*, a class that is not a set is a *proper class*.) For more on sets and classes, see, for example, Parsons (1974).

adequate for dealing with "normal" consequences. Yet, in principle, it is inadequate.

Evaluation. One limitation of this criticism is that it is specific to a particular background theory used to precisify various notions appearing in the semantic definition of LC, namely, ZFC or a similar set theory. But the semantic definition itself is independent of any specific precisification of these notions. In particular, it is not committed to any specific background theory. There is nothing in the idea of models as representations of formal possibilities that requires the use of a specific theory such as ZFC as background theory. And problems arising in one background theory may not arise in another. Take the type-theoretic background theory that Tarski originally used to precisify his ideas. In this background theory, as McGee noted, universes of models are not limited to proper sets. This is not to say that we ought to go back to a type-theoretic background theory. But a more suitable theory is an open possibility.

In evaluating the semantic definition, therefore, it is important to distinguish between the definition itself and its mathematical precisifications. When the main goal is to investigate the *mathematical* properties of logic, it is reasonable to identify logic with a certain mathematical precisification. But in a *philosophical* study of logic this distorts our understanding, leading us to attribute weaknesses or peculiarities of the mathematical background theory to logic itself. Of course, had the critics shown that it is impossible *in principle* to construct an adequate apparatus of models, this would be a serious problem, but this is not what they have shown (or even set out to show).

Furthermore, it is an open question whether the above criticism holds even with respect to the ZFC precisification of the semantic definition of LC. In principle, to accurately represent a situation with a feature F, a model does not have to have the feature F itself: It has to adequately represent a situation that has this feature, or more precisely, the relevant aspects of such a situation. McGee, indeed, suggested that this might be the case with set-theoretic models. In principle, we might be able to represent proper-class structures indirectly, by means of *especially large* set models, based on so-called *reflection principles*:[58]

> [According to r]*eflection principles* ... the universe of pure sets is so large and structurally variegated that every structural property of the universe as a whole [– a proper class –] is already exemplified at some ordinal level of the set-theoretic hierarchy. (McGee 2004: 379)

---

[58] For reflection principles, see, for example, Levy (1960) and Bagaria (2019).

The idea is that proper-class structures "reflect down" on, or can be represented by, certain very large sets. Accordingly, an apparatus of models that has models with such sets as their universes can adequately represent truth-in-the-world-of-sets. It is, however, an open question whether this indeed is the case.

Another reason to question the class–set criticism is that it is not clear whether there are, even in the mathematical world, proper-class structures. One of the possible lessons from the class-theoretic paradoxes (such as Russell's) is that there are no genuine proper-class structures: speaking about such structures is just a *façon de parler*. In that case, proper-class properties are not genuine formal properties, and the problem discussed above is not a genuine problem. This, too, is an open question.

We may conclude by saying that there is no conclusive evidence for the views that (i) the (mathematical) world contains proper classes, so an adequate model-theoretic apparatus must include models that represent such classes; (ii) proper classes cannot be represented by set models; and (iii) no appropriate background theory of formal structure can admit proper classes. It is an open question whether any of these views are warranted. Furthermore, there are strong reasons for believing that the adequacy of the semantic definition of LC is not dependent on a particular precisification of its principles (or a precisification in a particular background theory). Finally, the existence of a *perfect* mathematical background theory cannot be a necessary condition for the philosophical adequacy of a definition of LC.

6 Criticisms of the Isomorphism-Invariance Criterion of Logicality

Criticisms of the isomorphism-invariance criterion of logicality are largely divided into two kinds: (A) criticisms claiming that the criterion overgenerates; and (B) criticisms claiming that the criterion undergenerates. Most published criticisms fall under (A). These criticisms are also of two kinds: (a) criticisms that focus on mathematical features of the criterion and/or its ramifications for the relation between logic and mathematics; (b) criticisms that focus on natural-language examples of intuitively non-LCs (allegedly) sanctioned by the criterion. The former criticisms are sometimes accompanied by proposals for alternative criteria of logicality. Many of the (A) criticisms are motivated, at least to some extent, by the so-called standard first-order thesis, associated with Quine, which views standard first-order logic as the "chosen" logic. They are often associated with a pragmatist approach to logic, denying the need for a systematic theoretic criterion of logicality altogether. The pragmatist attitude is also associated with criticisms of type (B).

In evaluating these criticisms I will focus on several things: (i) their precise content; (ii) whether they challenge the very need for a theoretical, systematic criterion of logicality or the specific criterion described here; (iii) whether they challenge the ideas expressed by this criterion or only a particular mathematical precisification of these ideas in a particular background theory; (iv) whether they are correctly viewed as *criticisms* of this criterion or are just *additional requirements* on admissible/desirable logical systems; and (v) whether they concern this criterion as a necessary or as a sufficient criterion of logicality. Let us now turn to these criticisms.

6.1 Overgeneration

A. *Meta-Logical/Mathematical Criticisms*
(a) *The (Standard) First-Order Thesis (Quine)*

Quine did not consider the isomorphism-invariance criterion of logicality, but many criticisms of this criterion are motivated, or influenced, by a Quinean thesis. Barwise (1985: 5) called this thesis the *"first-order thesis,"* but a more accurate title is the *"standard* first-order thesis." This thesis says that standard first-order logic is the "chosen" logic, the only genuine logic, or the preferred logic. In Barwise's words, the thesis says that "logic is [standard] first-order logic, so that anything that cannot be defined in [standard] first-order logic is outside the domain of logic" (Barwise 1985: 5). In particular, none of the nonstandard constants satisfying the isomorphism-invariance criterion is genuinely logical.

Why is standard first-order logic the "chosen" logic? One source of this view, according to Barwise, is the "pervasive nominalism in the philosophy of science in the mid-twentieth century, led by Quine" (Barwise 1985: 5). Another source, I would add, is Quine's pragmatism. In *Philosophy of Logic* (1970/1986), Quine used considerations based on both these sources to reject extensions of standard first-order logic. On the one hand, he viewed extended logics as "[s]et theory in sheep's clothing" (Quine 1970/1986: 66), where set theory, here, represented "ontological excesses" (Quine 1970/1985: 68). On the other hand, he viewed the fact that standard first-order logic has a complete proof system as a pragmatic ground for favoring it. Quine's (standard) first-order thesis has been highly influential for many decades, but substantial theoretic justifications of this thesis are rare.

Evaluation. Quine's considerations for viewing standard first-order logic as the "chosen" logic are orthogonal to the considerations that motivated the isomorphism-invariance criterion of logicality in the context of the semantic definition of LC. Although Quine was familiar with Tarski's 1936 (1983 [1936a]) paper, as far as I know, he never mentioned the problem of ℓcs raised in this paper, never discussed the issue of a general criterion of logicality, and, with one exception, never considered any of the nonstandard ℓcs sanctioned by the isomorphism-invariance criterion of logicality. For these reasons, Quine's view of logicality is largely irrelevant for the present discussion and I will not dwell on it here. It is quite likely, however, that Quine's view played a significant role in motivating some criticisms of isomorphism-invariance in the current literature.

(b) *Feferman's Criticisms and Alternative Proposal*

Feferman (1999, 2010) offered three criticisms of the isomorphism-invariance criterion of logicality, which he directed at "the Tarski–Sher thesis": (i) "The thesis assimilates logic to mathematics, more specifically to set theory"; (ii) "The set-theoretical notions involved in explaining [the thesis] are not robust"; and (iii) "No natural explanation is given by [the thesis] of what constitutes the *same* logical operation over arbitrary basic domains" (Feferman 1999: 37). Before getting into these criticisms, let me mention some of the things that Feferman did not object to. Feferman did not object to the division of constants into logical and nonlogical. Nor did he object to a systematic criterion of logicality, a semantic criterion, the philosophical idea that logicality is formality, or the isomorphism-invariance criterion as a *necessary* condition of logicality. Furthermore, Feferman (in the aforementioned papers) advocated only a limited revision of the criterion. Nevertheless, Feferman was highly critical of the claim that the criterion is sufficient for logicality. This led him to propose an alternative criterion. Feferman's criticisms were seconded by Bonnay (2008) who, however, criticized Feferman's own criterion (and proposed an alternative). Both Feferman's criticisms and his criterion were criticized by Sher (e.g., 2008, 2016) and Griffiths and Paseau (2016, 2022). Let us begin with Feferman's criticisms.

(i) *The Tarski–Sher Thesis Assimilates Logic to Mathematics*

Feferman viewed the isomorphism-invariance criterion as leading to the assimilation of logic to mathematics, something he objected to. This objection was based on *intuitive*, rather than theoretical, considerations: "[this criticism] evidently depend-[s] on one's *gut feelings* about the nature of logic" (Feferman 1999: 37, my emphasis). In further elaborating his objection, Feferman appealed to Quinean nominalistic considerations as well: It is possible to "express ... many ... substantial mathematical propositions as logically determinate statements on the Tarski–Sher thesis" (Feferman 1999: 38). This indicates, according to Feferman, that the isomorphism-invariance criterion introduces existential commitments into logic – commitments to "the existence of set-theoretical entities of a special kind, or at least of their determinate properties" (Feferman 1999: 38). This makes it "evident that we have thereby transcended logic as the arena of universal notions independent of 'what there is'" (Feferman 1999: 38). One mathematical statement that can be expressed logically, given the isomorphism-invariance criterion, is the Continuum Hypothesis (CH), which says that the smallest infinite cardinal larger than $\aleph_0$, $\aleph_1$ equals $2^{\aleph_0}$. Assuming the isomorphism-invariance criterion, this mathematical hypothesis can be expressed without using any nonlogical mathematical constants, by, for example:

(13) $(2^{\aleph_0}x)x=x \equiv (\aleph_1 x)x=x.$

Here the quantifiers "$2^{\aleph_0}$" and "$\aleph_1$" are second-level logical predicates denoting the second-level formal properties EXACTLY-TWO-TO-THE-POWER-OF-ALEPH-NULL-MANY and EXACTLY-ALEPH-ONE-MANY.

Evaluation. (a) The relation between logic and mathematics has been a central topic of discussion in the philosophy of logic for a long time. As we have seen in Section 4.6, the view that logic and mathematics are identical, or one is included in the other, is associated with the *logicists*, who viewed mathematics as *reducible* to, hence included in, logic. But this is not the view associated with the isomorphism-invariance criterion. The view associated with it is that there is a systematic connection between logic and mathematics, but it is neither identity nor inclusion. Logic and mathematics are both grounded in the formal structure of the world, but there is a division of labor between them concerning the formal: mathematics *studies* the formal, logic *uses* our knowledge of the formal to construct a method of reasoning. Logic and mathematics develop in tandem, in a back-and-forth, Neurathian, manner: Mathematics uses logic as a framework and proof method for its theories; logic uses (the formal properties and laws studied by) mathematics as a basis for its $\mathcal{l}$cs and model-theoretic apparatus of LC.

This view of the relation between logic and mathematics is based on *theoretic* considerations, and as such it cannot be undermined by *gut feelings*, which are in any case unreliable and lack critical perspective. Someone might say that "we have to start somewhere" and "sometimes the only place to start is our gut feelings." But eventually we have to critically examine our gut feelings (e.g., using the holistic method described in Section 3.2), and in any case, gut feelings never provide genuine justification/refutation of a philosophical view.

(b) The logical expressibility of mathematical statements is not specific to the generalized logics sanctioned by the isomorphism-invariance criterion: Standard first-order logic already expresses the content of infinitely many mathematical statements. For example, every arithmetical statement of the form "k+m=n," where k, m, and n are natural numbers, is expressible in standard first-order logic by a sentence of the (abbreviated) form

(14) $[(k!x)\Phi x \ \& \ (m!x)\Psi x \ \& \ \sim(\exists x)(\Phi x \& \Psi x)] \supset (n!x)(\Phi x \vee \Psi x)]$,

where "k!/m!/n!" means "exactly k/m/n."[59]

In this connection, it is worthwhile to note that being expressible exclusively by ℓcs is not the same thing as being logically true. Some schemas and sentences with purely logical vocabulary, such as

(15) $(\exists x)x \neq x$

are logically false, and some, like

(16) $(n!x)x=x$

are logically indeterminate. Others, like

(17) $[(1!x)\Phi x \ \& \ (2!x)\Psi x \ \& \ \sim(\exists x)(\Phi x \& \Psi x)] \supset (3!x)(\Phi x \vee \Psi x)]$

are logically true. (17) is a genuine logical truth whose numerical quantifiers are all defined from the primitive ℓcs of standard first-order logic, and as such it is a standard first-order logical truth.

(c) The logical truth of sentences like (17) does not commit standard first-order logic to the existence of numerical individuals (numbers). (17) commits standard first-order logic to certain *formal relations* between the cardinality *properties* EXACTLY-ONE, EXACTLY-TWO, EXACTLY-THREE. But it does not commit it to the *existence* of the *individuals* 1, 2, and 3, or any other mathematical *individuals*. The same holds for all logical truths, standard or generalized, expressing mathematical content, including (13). If, and to the extent that, we assume bivalence, (13), like (17), is formally, hence logically, true or false. Which one it is we at present do not know. But regardless of whether it is formally (logically) true or false, (13) does not commit us to the existence of the mathematical individuals $2^{\aleph_0}$ or $\aleph_1$ any more than (17) commits us to the existence of 1, 2, or 3. The ontological commitments of logics incorporating isomorphism-invariant ℓcs – either standard or generalized – *are different* from those of (standard first-order) mathematics.[60]

---

[59] For example, "$(2!x)\Phi x$" is defined by "$(\exists x)(\exists y)[(\Phi x \& \Phi y \& x \neq y) \& (\forall z)(\Phi z \supset (z=x \vee z=y))]$."

[60] (i) In this context, see the conception of mathematics sketched in the last paragraph of Section 4.6(c), where mathematical individuals are conceived as posits representing higher-level formal properties.

(ii) For further ways in which the logical expressibility of mathematical statements (e.g., CH) fails to undermine the isomorphism-invariance criterion of logicality, see Griffith and Paseau (2016, 2022).

Let us now turn to Feferman's second criticism:

(ii) The Tarski–Sher Thesis Sanctions Nonrobust (Nonabsolute) ℓcs

Feferman argued that logic should sanction only ℓcs whose standard first-order set-theoretic correlates are robust. By that he meant that they "have the same meaning independent of the exact extent of the set-theoretical universe" (Feferman 1999: 38). The concept of robustness Feferman precisified using the meta-set-theoretic notion of *absoluteness*. This notion is usually traced to Gödel, who introduced it in an altogether different context, but it has been extended beyond this context. In the present context, Feferman defined absoluteness as:

> Let T be a set of axioms in the language of set theory. A formula ϕ of set theory is defined to be *absolute with respect to T* if ϕ is invariant under end-extensions for models of T. (Feferman 2010: 13)

How is this relevant to logic? How is it relevant to ℓcs that are for the most part second-level predicates, hence different in level from the first-level predicates identified with first-order set-theoretic formulas? Feferman did not say, but it is reasonable to presume that he assumed second-level logical predicates are defined within a standard first-order background set theory.

What is the general significance of absoluteness? Väänänen explains the general idea behind absoluteness as follows:

> Intuitively speaking, a concept is absolute if its meaning is independent of the formalism used, or in other words, if its meaning in the formal sense is the same as its meaning in the "real world." (Väänänen 2019: section 6)

A natural way to understand this idea is through the Löwenheim–Skolem theorem (see Section 4.7). This theorem implies that in spite of the fact that standard first-order set theory says that there are uncountably-many sets, it has a countable model, that is, a model with only countably-many sets in its universe.[61] In this model, the standard first-order set-theoretic statement

(18) There are uncountably-many sets

is true. Clearly, the standard first-order predicate "uncountably-many" has a different meaning in this model than its "real" meaning.

Now, according to the isomorphism-invariance criterion, the first-level "uncountably-many" is a *non-ℓc*, but its second-level correlate, the quantifier

---

[61] Recall: In standard first-order set theory sets are individuals.

"UNCOUNTABLY-MANY," is *logical*. This quantifier, however, is defined within standard first-order set theory in terms of the first-level predicate "uncountably-many," which is nonabsolute, and that, Feferman said, rules it out as an admissible ℓc. Some nonstandard logical quantifiers sanctioned by the isomorphism-invariance criterion are absolute: for example, "is-finite" and "is-well-founded" (Feferman 1999, 2010), but some are not. This, according to Feferman, disqualifies the isomorphism-invariance criterion from being an adequate criterion of logicality.

It should be noted that different logicians hold different views about the significance of absoluteness. Thus, Barwise said:

> One should not fall into the trap of thinking of absolute logics as somehow better than [non-absolute] logics, any more than one would think of fields as better than rings. (Barwise 1972: 314)

And Feferman himself noted that the notion of absoluteness is not absolute:

> One should be aware that the notion of absoluteness is itself relative, and is sensitive to a background set theory, hence again to the question of what entities exist. (Feferman 1999: 38)

Evaluation. The absoluteness criticism raises questions concerning what is relevant and what is not relevant to logicality. Neither Feferman nor, as far as I know, any other critic who appealed to absoluteness addressed its relevance to logicality. Is having a first-level nonlogical correlate that is not absolute an appropriate reason for concluding that a given second-level constant is nonlogical? Does absoluteness have anything to do with the distinctive traits of ℓcs and LC, namely, formality for the former and formal necessity for the latter? The issue of nonabsoluteness has been imported to the topic of logicality without a clear rationale.

Another problematic aspect of the absoluteness criticism, which it shares with some criticisms of the semantic definition of LC (see Section 5.2), is that it is specific to a particular background theory of logic, namely standard first-order set theory. We have already seen that this theory is no more than an *optional* background theory, and some (e.g., Griffiths and Paseau, 2022) suggest that the isomorphism-invariance criterion can avoid this criticism by using second-order set theory as its background theory. But even if we continue to use standard first-order set theory as our background theory, it is not clear whether the absoluteness criticism applies. This depends on how, exactly, a given background theory is involved in determining the meanings of the ℓcs. Let us now turn to this question.

When we apply the isomorphism-invariance criterion to, say, the second-level predicate-quantifier "UNCOUNTABLY-MANY," we are interested in the "real" meaning of this predicate-quantifier. Now, we know that standard first-order set theory has both models that capture its "real" meaning and models that do not (the latter include its countable Löwenheim–Skolem models). Which model of set theory should we use to define the meaning of "UNCOUNTABLY-MANY"? Clearly, we should use one of the former models. More generally, we use models that capture the real, or intended, meaning of the set-theoretic notions. But with respect to these models, the issue of absoluteness does not arise. This is another point the absoluteness critics did not address.

I should add that it is a bit ironic that the absoluteness problem is used to rule out a criterion that enables us to overcome this very problem. The absoluteness problem, as well as the Löwenheim–Skolem phenomenon related to it, arise only for formal notions defined within expressively weak logical frameworks, such as that of standard first-order logic. As the Löwenheim–Skolem theorem teaches us, this logical system is too weak to discern the formal difference between arbitrarily large finite collections of objects and infinite collections of objects, and as such cannot exploit the full richness of the apparatus of models, making essential use only of finite (including arbitrarily large finite) models but not of infinite models, let alone models of higher infinities. By adding to the language of standard first-order logic appropriate *l*cs sanctioned by the isomorphism-invariance criterion, we avoid the problem: We obtain a stronger first-order logic, and a stronger first-order set theory using it as its logical framework, blocking the downward Löwneheim–Skolem theorem and nonabsoluteness.

Finally, it is important to distinguish between the requirement of logicality and other requirements that one may wish to set on logical systems/constants. Thus, if one is interested in completeness, one may decide to limit oneself to complete logical systems, in which case, one will admit standard first-order logic as well as Keisler's first-order generalized logic with its logical quantifier "UNCOUNTABLY-MANY," but not all generalized logics. Similarly, if one is interested in absoluteness, one may limit oneself to logical systems with *l*cs whose nonlogical set-theoretic correlates are absolute, thus rejecting Keisler's logic but accepting logics with the generalized logical quantifier "IS-WELL-FOUNDED." In both cases, one is interested in issues that are quite different from the one associated with the logicality problem raised by the semantic definition of LC, and so one sets *additional* requirements, *over and above* the requirement that logicality capture the essential features of logic (LC), formality and necessity.

Feferman's last criticism is:

(iii) *"Sameness" of *l*cs*

The isomorphism-invariance criterion sanctions any formal constant as an admissible *l*c. But some formal constants behave in ways that are intuitively bizarre. For example, one admissible logical quantifier behaves like "∀" in finite universes and like "∃" in infinite universes. Feferman argues that such a logical quantifier lacks internal unity: It is not clear what makes it "the same quantifier." In his words:

> It seems to me there is a sense in which the usual operations of the first-order predicate calculus have the *same meaning* independent of the domain of individuals over which they are applied. This characteristic is *not* captured by invariance under bijections. As McGee puts it "The Tarski-Sher thesis does not require that there be any connections among the ways a logical operation acts on domains of different sizes." (Feferman 1999: 38)

Evaluation. This phenomenon is not specific to nonstandard logics sanctioned by the isomorphism-invariance criterion. All reasonable logics sanction ℓcs of this kind. Thus, standard first-order logic has a logical quantifier (defined from the standard logical quantifiers) that behaves like "∀" in universes of cardinality ≤1007 and like "∃" in universes of cardinality >1007.

Furthermore, it is important to note that the quantifiers in question are sensitive only to *formal* features of universes of model. The isomorphism-invariance criterion does not sanction quantifiers that behave like "∀" in universes of wombats and like "∃" in universes of nonwombats. The quantifiers it sanctions are all formal, and as such give rise to genuinely logical, that is, formal-and-necessary (formally necessary) LCs.[62]

Finally, it is very common that notions ranging over large numbers of objects, such as "real number" or "set", have very bizarre and disorderly instances, ones that may seem as if they lack internal unity. Indeed, Feferman himself recognized that many mathematical objects are "monst[rous]" or "pathological" (Feferman 2000: 317) yet are perfectly legitimate. There does not seem to be a reason why the notion of formal property/constant, which underlies the isomorphism-invariance conception of a logical property/constant, should not share this feature.

Feferman, as noted earlier, proposed an alternative criterion of logicality. Let us now turn to this criterion.

(iv) *Homomorphism-Invariance Criterion of Logicality*

---

[62] Note that the *fixity* of logical constants/properties/operators is compatible with their behaving like "∀" in universes of one cardinality and like "∃" in universes of other cardinalities. Indeed, even ∀ is of this kind: It behaves like the quantifier "EXACTLY-TEN" in universes of cardinality TEN and like "EXACTLY-ELEVEN" in universes of cardinality ELEVEN. A logical operator is fixed in the sense that it behaves in the same way in all formally identical circumstances. It is prefixed in the sense that its denotation is determined in advance (or independently) of the individuals and nonlogical denotations of a given model.

Feferman proposed an alternative criterion of logicality, one that limits the range of ℓcs compared to the isomorphism-invariance criterion. Like the latter, Feferman's criterion is an invariance criterion, but instead of requiring that logical properties/constants be invariant under all *isomorphisms*, it requires that they be invariant under all *homomorphisms*. A homomorphism of two structures, $<D_1,\beta_1>$ and $<D_2,\beta_2>$ is, here, a function h from D_1 onto D_2 (which is not necessarily 1–1) that preserves relations, that is, β_2 is the image in D_2 of β_1 under h. Since the requirement of homomorphism is weaker than that of isomorphism, there are more homomorphisms than isomorphisms,[63] and as a result, fewer constants satisfy the requirement of being invariant under all homomorphisms than being invariant under all isomorphisms. In particular, cardinality quantifiers such as "exactly κ," $\kappa > 0$, are not invariant under all homomorphisms and as such are ruled out as logical quantifiers. Other invariance criteria that restrict the scope of ℓcs were also proposed (e.g., by Bonnay 2008), but since the problems they raise are not altogether different from the ones discussed below with respect to Feferman's criterion, I limit my discussion to the latter.

Evaluation. Feferman's criterion appears to overshoot, even by his own lights. It rules out not just nonstandard ℓcs sanctioned by the isomorphism-invariance criterion, but also standard ℓcs, such as finite cardinality quantifiers ("AT-LEAST/EXACTLY/AT-MOST-n," for finite n's>1). Feferman was aware of this problem and considered ways to avoid it (e.g., by removing "=," just for this reason, from the list of standard ℓcs). This, however, would result in an ad hoc criterion.

Indeed, even without such adjustments, the criterion appears to be ad hoc. Unlike the isomorphism-invariance criterion, which is associated with a clear, philosophically motivated, conception of logicality (namely, logicality as formality, where the latter is characterized by isomorphism-invariance), the homomorphism-invariance criterion is not associated (or at least has not been shown, or even claimed, to be associated) with any such conception.

Intuitively, too, the homomorphism criterion is problematic. While some of the standard ℓcs come out nonlogical, nonstandard quantifiers such as "IS-WELL-FOUNDED" come out logical. One is hard pressed to explain this in a way that makes either philosophically or mathematically intuitive sense.[64]

---

[63] "More" in the sense of inclusion.

[64] For a proposal of a joint proof-theoretic–semantic criterion of ℓcs (partly based on a suggestion made by Feferman, who eventually gave up his homomorphism criterion), see Speitel (2020).

B. *Linguistic Criticisms*

Several philosophers criticized the isomorphism-invariance criterion on grounds that have to do with natural language. These critics usually pointed to constants that allegedly satisfy the isomorphism-invariance criterion of logicality yet give rise to consequences (truths, falsehoods) that are intuitively nonlogical. Some of these critics prefer a pragmatist approach to logicality over a systematic theoretic approach.

Examples:

(i)   McCarthy (1981) claims that the isomorphism-invariance criterion classifies some constants whose content is contingent as logical. Such constants give rise to consequences that are supposedly logical yet are contingent. Consider "THE-NUMBER-OF-MOONS-(OF-EARTH)." This constant denotes the same second-level property as the ℓc "EXACTLY-ONE," and as such it satisfies the isomorphism-invariance criterion. But it denotes this property only contingently. As a result, it gives rise to consequences like

(19) (NUMBER-OF-MOONS x)Φx; therefore, ~(EXACTLY-TWO x)Φx,

which are supposedly logical, yet are contingent. This undermines the isomorphism-invariance criterion.[65]

(ii) Consider the quantifier Q*, which behaves like ∃ in universes that have fewer members than the least number n of whole seconds in which, up through to the end of the twenty-first century, a human being runs a mile, and like ∀ in all other universes. This quantifier, according to Hanson (1997), satisfies the isomorphism-invariance criterion but is a nonsuitable candidate for an ℓc for two reasons: (1) It is unnatural for an ℓc to behave in one way in one universe and in another way in another. (2) This constant does not satisfy the requirement that LC not "be influenced in any way by empirical knowledge" (Tarski 1983 [1936a]: 414). On both grounds, a criterion that classifies Q* as an ℓc is a flawed criterion.

(iii) According to Gómez-Torrente (2002), the predicate "is-a-male-widow" satisfies the invariance-isomorphism criterion since it is necessarily coextensional with the genuine ℓc "is-not-self-identical." As such, it gives rise to the supposedly logical truth

(20) (∀x)~ Male-Widow x.

But intuitively (20) is not a *logical* truth.

---

[65] One may argue that even a predicate such as "IS-NONEMPTY-AND-WATER-IS-H_2O," which (if Kripke 1970/1980 is right), is necessarily equivalent to "IS-NONEMPTY," should not be considered logical (see MacFarlane 2015).

Rebuttals of these criticisms can be found in Sher (1991, 2001, 2003, 2021), Sagi (2015), and Griffiths and Paseau (2022). Discussing all of these rebuttals, however, will divert us from our main task. Here I will limit myself to several points, focusing on whether the constants introduced in the above examples are indeed logical according to the isomorphism-invariance criterion of logicality and why.

Evaluation. (i) "THE-NUMBER-OF-MOONS-(OF-EARTH)": two approaches to constants of this kind that are compatible with the isomorphism-invariance criterion are: (A) We approach them extensionally in the sense of disregarding the contingency of their denotation, that is, we identify their denotation (in all domains) with their actual denotation. In other words, we treat "THE-NUMBER-OF-MOONS" as *synonymous* with "EXACTLY-ONE." As a result, "THE-NUMBER-OF-MOONS" (so understood!) is an ℓc, and a nonproblematic one. (B) We approach constants of this kind intensionally in the sense of taking into account the contingency of their denotation. We then check whether they satisfy the isomorphism-invariance criterion. They do not. Let D_1 be $\{m_1, a, b\}$ and D_2 be $\{m_1, m_2, c\}$, where m_1 is the actual moon of Earth, m_2 is a counterfactual moon of Earth, and a, b, and c are some actual-counterfactual individuals that are not moons of Earth. In D_1 (structures with D_1 as their domain), THE-NUMBER-OF-MOONS is EXACTLY-ONE; in D_2 (structures with D_2 as their domain), THE-NUMBER-OF-MOONS is EXACTLY-TWO. Now take the structures $S_1 = <D_1, P_{D1}>$, $S_2 = <D_2, P_{D2}>$, where $P_{D1} = \{a\}$, $P_{D2} = \{c\}$. $S_1 \cong S_2$, but P_{D1} satisfies "NUMBER-OF-MOONS" in S_1 while P_{D2} does not satisfy "NUMBER-OF-MOONS" in S_2. Hence, "NUMBER-OF-MOONS" is not an ℓc. Either way ((A) or (B) approach), this case does not undermine the isomorphism-invariance criterion.[66]

(ii) Q*: concerning criticism (1) – unnaturalness – we have already explained why naturalness has nothing to do with logicality (see discussion of Feferman in (A) earlier). Concerning criticism (2) – contingency – we can approach it in the two ways we approached (i) earlier: (A) extensional approach. Here there is a definite number n that determines what Q* is, and the fact that we have to wait until the end of the twenty-first century to know what n is is irrelevant to logicality. (B) intensional approach: Here Q* is not isomorphism-invariant. For any two formally possible running

---

[66] Concerning "IS-NONEMPTY-AND-WATER-IS-H2O," this predicate is not *formally* equivalent to "IS-NONEMPTY," hence it is not logical.

speeds, there are domains with (formally possible) humans that run a mile in those speeds, and Q* is not invariant under all isomorphisms of structures with such domains.

(iii) The impossibility of being a male widow (like the impossibility of being both all-red and blue, see Section 3.4) is *not a formal* impossibility. Therefore, there are structures in which some formally possible individuals are male widows, and "is-a-male-widow" is nonempty in such domains, hence cannot be identified with "is-not-self-identical." In short, "is-a-male-widow" is not invariant under all isomorphisms of structures (with domains of formally possible individuals).

Finally, these criticisms are not really criticisms of the isomorphism-invariance criterion of logicality (but of which kind of equivalence counts). They are independent of the isomorphism-invariance criterion because each of the constants whose logicality is questioned by these criticisms is, if logical, a defined ℓc of *standard first-order logic*.

6.2 Undergeneration

The undergeneration criticism focuses on the fact that the isomorphism-invariance criterion does not classify the distinctive operators of "nonmathematical" logics – such as modal logic – as logical. The claim is that since in practice we do regard modal systems as logical, the isomorphism-invariance criterion (or its sentential correlate) undergenerates. An adequate criterion of logicality should be satisfied by all constants that are *in practice* treated as logical. There is nothing more to such a criterion than tracking our current practices (see, e.g., Dutilh Novaes 2014).

Evaluation. The isomorphism-invariance criterion of logicality is not intended to be a purely descriptive criterion, one that simply describes our current practices. To identify the constants that are commonly treated as logical in current practice, all we need is a list. The isomorphism-invariance criterion is a *theoretic*, systematic criterion, designed to solve a certain theoretic problem and do so in a critical manner and unchained by existent customs and conventions. It is intended to be a *critical* criterion for a certain basic type of logic: general predicate logic. And the theoretical problem it sets out to solve is the selection of ℓcs, guided by the goal of identifying all and only *formal-and-necessary* consequences as logical.

The isomorphism-invariance criterion offers a solution to this problem, using the fruitful idea of invariance. It follows from this solution that (i) the ℓcs of standard first-order logic are logical, and (ii) they are not the only ℓcs.

The criterion, as we have emphasized, is designed for formal, mathematical logic, which is widely recognized as a very basic type of logic. In focusing on this type of logic, it does not pass a negative judgment on any other type of logic, such as modal logic, whose semantic apparatus differs from that of mathematical logic in including possible worlds, accessibility relations, frames, and so on. The project of critically examining such logics, understanding their task or function, providing them with a philosophical grounding, characterizing their distinguished constants, and examining their relation to formal (mathematical) logic is a different project from the one studied in this Element and a welcome addition to it.

7 Conclusion

In this Element we have engaged in an in-depth study of LC, focused on its semantic definition. Starting with Tarski's classical (1983 [1936a]) paper, we have examined the character of semantics in general and logical semantics in particular, the route from the semantic definition of truth to the semantic definition of LC, the fundamental conditions of necessity and formality on an adequate definition of LC, the attempts to construct a semantic definition satisfying these conditions, and the challenges facing the construction of a definition of this kind, including the problem of logicality (ℓcs). We described the isomorphism-invariance criterion of logicality and explained how it resolves this problem. We have further explained how isomorphism-invariance is connected to formality, and how formality, in turn, is connected to an especially strong type of necessity (formal necessity) as well as to other desired features of LC such as topic neutrality, generality, strong normativity, and so on. We explained the model-theoretic apparatus used in the semantic definition of LC: what models represent; the definition of truth-in-a-model; how preservation-of-truth-in-all-models is tantamount to formal-and-necessary preservation of truth; and more. We have shown that the standard first-order notion of LC is theoretically adequate, but we have also shown that it does not exhaust the formal notion of LC, and explained how, and how far, it can be extended. We have explained how logic is grounded in the *formal* structure of the world and discussed the relation between logic and mathematics. And we have analyzed, evaluated, and clarified criticisms and confusions concerning the semantic definition of LC and the associated criterion of logicality. We have further discussed the philosophical grounding of the semantic conception of LC in the human pursuit of knowledge and its ramifications for logicality.

There is a large variety of additional conceptions of LC in the philosophical literature. Those of intrinsic interest include (but are not limited to) the inferentialist conception (e.g. Brandom 1994, Peregrin 2014), the intuitionist conception (see, e.g., Posy 2020), the cognitive-economy conception (e.g., Field 2015), the neo-Tarskian pragmatist conception (e.g., Varzi 2002), the logical nihilist conception (e.g., Russell 2018), the logical deflationist conception (e.g., L. Shapiro 2011), and the logical pluralist conception (e.g., Beall and Restall 2006, S. Shapiro 2014). We have briefly touched upon a few of these, but our goal of an in-depth philosophical understanding together with limitations on length led us to focus on one highly significant conception, the *semantic* conception of LC in the core system of formal logic.

References

Bagaria, J. 2019. "Set Theory." *Stanford Encyclopedia of Philosophy.* E. N. Zalta (ed.). Stanford, CA: The Metaphysics Research Lab.

Barwise, J. 1972. "Absolute Logics and $L_{\infty\,\omega}$." *Annals of Mathematical Logic* 4: 309–340.

    1985. "Model-Theoretic Logics: Background and Aims." *Model-Theoretic Logics.* J. Barwise and S. Feferman (eds.). New York: Springer-Verlag. pp. 3–23.

Beall, J. C., and G. Restall. 2006. *Logical Pluralism.* Oxford: Oxford University Press.

Bonnay, D. 2008. "Logicality and Invariance." *Bulletin of Symbolic Logic* 14: 29–68.

Brandom, R. B. 1994. *Making It Explicit.* Cambridge, MA: Harvard University Press.

Chihara, C. 1998. "Tarski's Thesis and the Ontology of Mathematics." *The Philosophy of Mathematics Today.* M. Schirn (ed.). Oxford: Oxford University Press. pp. 157–172.

Dummett, M. 1978. *Truth and Other Enigmas.* Cambridge, MA: Harvard University Press.

Dutilh Novaes, C. 2014. "The Undergeneration of Permutation Invariance as a Criterion for Logicality." *Erkenntnis* 79: 81–97.

Enderton, H. B. 2001. *A Mathematical Introduction to Logic.* San Diego, CA: Hartcourt.

Etchemendy, J. 1990. *The Concept of Logical Consequence.* Cambridge, MA: Harvard University Press.

    2008. "Reflections on Consequence." *New Essays on Tarski and Philosophy.* D. Patterson (ed.). Oxford: Oxford University Press. pp. 263–299.

Feferman, S. 1999. "Logic, Logics, and Logicism." *Notre Dame Journal of Formal Logic* 40: 31–54.

    2000. "Mathematical Intuition vs. Mathematical Monsters." *Synthese* 125: 317–322.

    2010. "Set-theoretical Invariance Criteria for Logicality." *Notre Dame Journal of Formal Logic* 51: 3–20.

Field, H. 2009. "What Is the Normative Role of Logic?" *Proceedings of the Aristotelian Society* Suppl. 83: 251–268.

    2015. "What Is Logical Validity." *Foundations of Logical Consequence.* C. R. Caret and O. T. Hjortland (eds.). Oxford: Oxford University Press. pp. 33–70.

Fitting, M. 2015. "Intensional Logic." *Stanford Encyclopedia of Philosophy*. E. N. Zalta (ed.). Stanford, CA: The Metaphysics Research Lab.

Frege, G. 1967 (1879). "Begriffsschrift." *From Frege to Gödel*. J. van Heijenoort (ed.). Cambridge, MA: Harvard University Press. pp. 5–82.

1893. *The Basic Laws of Arithmetic*. Vol. 1. Berkeley, CA: University of California Press, English translation 1964.

1918. "Thoughts." *Logical Investigations*. Oxford: Basil Blackwell, English translation 1977. pp. 1–30.

Friedman, M. 2001. *Dynamics of Reason*. Stanford, CA: CSLI.

García-Carpintero, M. 1993. "The Grounds of the Model-theoretic Account of the Logical Properties." *Notre Dame Journal of Formal Logic* 34: 107–131.

Gödel, K. 1986 (1929). "On the Completeness of the Calculus of Logic." *Collected Works*. Vol. 1. S. Feferman, J. W. Dawson, Jr., S. C. Kleene, et al. (eds.). New York: Oxford University Press. pp. 61–101.

1986 (1931). "On Formally Undecidable Propositions of *Principia Mathematica* and Related Systems I." *Collected Works*. Vol. 1. S. Feferman, J. D. Dawson, Jr., S. C. Kleene, et al. (eds.). New York: Oxford University Press. pp. 145–195.

Gómez-Torrente, M. 1996. "Tarski on Logical Consequence." *Notre Dame Journal of Formal Logic* 37: 125–151.

2002. "The Problem of Logical Constants." *Bulletin of Symbolic Logic* 8: 1–37.

Griffiths, O., and A. C. Paseau. 2016. "Isomorphism Invariance and Overgeneration." *Bulletin of Symbolic Logic* 22: 482–503.

2022. *One True Logic*. Oxford: Oxford University Press.

Hanson, W. H. 1997. "The Concept of Logical Consequence." *Philosophical Review* 106: 365–409.

Harman, G. 1986. *Change in View*. Cambridge, MA: The MIT Press.

Hilbert, D. 1950 (1899). *The Foundations of Geometry*. La Salle, IL: Open Court.

Hilbert, D., and W. Ackerman. 1950 (1928). *Principles of Mathematical Logic*. New York: Chelsea Publishing.

Hodges, W. 1986. "Truth in a Structure." *Proceedings of the Aristotelian Society* 86: 135–151.

Jacquette, D. 1994. "Tarski's Quantificational Semantics and Meinongian Object Theory Domains." *Pacific Philosophical Quarterly* 75: 88–107.

Kant, I. 1929 (1781/1787). *Critique of Pure Reason*. London: Macmillan.

Keisler, H. J. 1970. "Logic with the Quantifier 'There Exist Uncountably Many.'" *Annals of Mathematical Logic* 1: 1–93.

Klein, F. 1872. "A Comparative Review of Recent Researches in Geometry." PhD thesis. University of Bonn.

Kreisel, G. 1967. "Informal Rigor and Completeness Proofs." *Problems in the Philosophy of Mathematics*. I. Lakatos (ed.). Amsterdam: North-Holland. pp. 138–186.

Kripke, S. 1970/1980. *Naming and Necessity*. Cambridge, MA: Harvard University Press.

Levy, A. 1960. "Axiom Schemata of Strong Infinity in Axiomatic Set Theory." *Pacific Journal of Mathematics* 10: 223–238.

Lindström, P. 1966. "First Order Predicate Logic with Generalized Quantifiers." *Theoria* 32: 186–195.

1969. "On Extensions of Elementary Logic." *Theoria* 35: 1–11.

Löwenheim, L. 1967 (1915). "On Possibilities in the Calculus of Relatives." *From Frege to Gödel*. J. van Heijenoort (ed.). Cambridge, MA: Harvard University Press. pp. 228–251.

MacFarlane, J. 2000. "What Does It Mean to Say That Logic Is Formal?" PhD thesis. University of Pittsburgh.

2015. "Logical Constants." *Stanford Encyclopedia of Philosophy*. E. N. Zalta (ed.). Stanford, CA: The Metaphysics Research Lab.

Maddy, P. 2007. *Second Philosophy*. Oxford: Oxford University Press.

May, R. 1985. *Logical Form: Its Structure and Derivation*. Cambridge, MA: The MIT Press.

McCarthy, T. 1981. "The Idea of a Logical Constant." *Journal of Philosophy* 78: 499–523.

McGee, V. 1992a. "Review of Etchemendy, The Concept of Logical Consequence." *Journal of Symbolic Logic* 57: 254–255.

1992b. "Two Problems with Tarski's Theory of Consequence." *Proceedings of the Aristotelian Society* 92: 273–292.

1996. "Logical Operations." *Journal of Philosophical Logic* 25: 567–580.

2004. "Tarski's Staggering Existential Assumptions." *Synthese* 142: 371–387.

Montague, R. 1974. "The Proper Treatment of Quantification in Ordinary English." *Formal Philosophy: Selected Papers*. R. H. Thomason (ed.). New Haven, CT: Yale University Press. pp. 247–270.

Mostowski, A. 1957. "On a Generalization of Quantifiers." *Fundamenta Mathematicae* 44: 12–36.

Parsons, C. 1974. "Sets and Classes." *Noûs* 8: 1–12.

Peregrin, J. 2014. *Inferentialism: Why Rules Matter*. London: Palgrave-Macmillan.

Peters, S., and D. Westerståhl. 2006. *Quantifiers in Language and Logic*. Oxford: Oxford University Press.

Posy, C. 2020. *Mathematical Intuitionism*. Cambridge: Cambridge University Press.

Priest, G. 1995. "Etchemendy and Logical Consequence." *Canadian Journal of Philosophy* 25: 283–292.

Quine, W. V. 1970/1986. *Philosophy of Logic*. Cambridge, MA: Harvard University Press.

Ray, G. 1996. "Logical Consequence: A Defense of Tarski." *Journal of Philosophical Logic* 25: 303–313.

Rescher, N. 1962. "Plurality-Quantification." Abstract. *Journal of Symbolic Logic* 27: 373–374.

Resnik, M. D. 1981. "Mathematics as a Science of Patterns: Ontology and Reference." *Noûs* 15: 529–550.

Russell, B. 1971 (1919). *Introduction to Mathematical Philosophy*. New York: Simon & Schuster.

Russell, G. 2018. "Logical Nihilism: Could There Be No Logic?" *Philosophical Issues* 28: 308–324.

  2020. "Logic Isn't Normative." *Inquiry* 63: 371–388.

Sagi, G. 2015. "The Modal and Epistemic Arguments against the Invariance Criterion for Logical Terms." *Journal of Philosophy* 112: 159–167.

Schurz, G. 1994. "Logical Truth: Comments on Etchemendy's Critique of Tarski." *Sixty Years of Tarski's Definition of Truth*. B. Twardowski and J. Woleński (eds.). Kraków: Philed. pp. 78–95.

Shapiro, L. 2011. "Deflating Logical Consequence." *Philosophical Quarterly* 61: 320–342.

Shapiro, S. 1997. *Philosophy of Mathematics*. Oxford: Oxford University Press.

  1998. "Logical Consequence: Models and Reality." *The Philosophy of Mathematics Today*. M. Schirn (ed.). Oxford: Oxford University Press. pp. 131–156.

  2014. *Varieties of Logic*. Oxford: Oxford University Press.

Sher, G. 1991. *The Bounds of Logic*. Cambridge, MA: The MIT Press.

  1996. "Did Tarski Commit 'Tarski's Fallacy'?" *Journal of Symbolic Logic* 61: 653–686.

  2001. "The Formal-structural View of Logical Consequence." *Philosophical Review* 110: 241–261.

  2003. "A Characterization of Logical Constants Is Possible." *Theoria* 18: 189–197.

  2008. "Tarski's Thesis." *New Essays on Tarski and Philosophy*. D. Patterson (ed.). Oxford: Oxford University Press. pp. 300–339.

  2016. *Epistemic Friction: An Essay on Knowledge, Truth, and Logic*. Oxford: Oxford University Press.

2021. "Invariance and Logicality in Perspective." *The Semantic Conception of Logic: Essays on Consequence, Invariance, and Meaning*. G. Sagi and J. Woods (eds.). Cambridge: Cambridge University Press.

Skolem, T. 1967 (1920). "A Simplified Proof of a Theorem by L. Löwenheim and Generalizations of the Theorem." *From Frege to Gödel*. J. van Heijenoort (ed.). Cambridge, MA: Harvard University Press. pp. 252–263.

Speitel, S. 2020. *Logical Constants between Inference and Reference: An Essay in the Philosophy of Logic*. PhD thesis. University of California–San Diego.

Steinberger, F. 2019. "Three Ways in Which Logic Might Be Normative." *Journal of Philosophy* 116: 5–31.

Tarski, A. 1966/1986. "What Are Logical Notions?" *History and Philosophy of Logic* 7: 143–154.

1983 (1933). "The Concept of Truth in Formalized Languages." *Logic, Semantics, Metamathematics*. J. Corcoran (ed.). Indianapolis, IN: Hackett. pp. 152–278.

1983 (1936a). "On the Concept of Logical Consequence." *Logic, Semantics, Metamathematics*. J. Corcoran (ed.). Indianapolis, IN: Hackett. pp. 409–420.

1983 [1936b]. "The Establishment of Scientific Semantics." *Logic, Semantics, Metamathematics*. J. Corcoran (ed.). Indianapolis, IN: Hackett. pp. 401–408.

Tarski, A., and R. L. Vaught. 1957. "Arithmetical Extensions of Relational Systems." *Compositio Mathematica* 13: 81–102.

Väänänen, J. 2019. "Second-order and Higher-order Logic." *Stanford Encyclopedia of Philosophy*. E. N. Zalta (ed.). Stanford, CA: The Metaphysics Research Lab.

Varzi, A. C. 2002. "On Logical Relativity." *Philosophical Issues* 12: 197–219.

Vaught, R. L. 1974. "Model Theory before 1945." L. Henkin, J. Addison, C. C. Chang, et al. (eds.). *Proceedings of the Tarski Symposium*. Providence, RI: American Mathematical Society. pp. 153–172.

Whitehead, A. N., and B. Russell. 1910–1913/1925–1927. *Principia Mathematica*. Vols. I–III. Cambridge: Cambridge University Press.

Acknowledgments

I would like to thank the students in my 2021 and 2022 classes on logical consequence, Milana Kostic, Brad Armour-Garb, Fred Kroon, Peter Sher, and two anonymous referees for valuable help in preparing the manuscript.

Cambridge Elements ☰

Philosophy and Logic

Bradley Armour-Garb

SUNY Albany

Brad Armour-Garb is chair and Professor of Philosophy at SUNY Albany. His books include *The Law of Non-Contradiction* (co-edited with Graham Priest and J. C. Beall, 2004), *Deflationary Truth* and *Deflationism and Paradox* (both co-edited with J. C. Beall, 2005), *Pretense and Pathology* (with James Woodbridge, Cambridge University Press, 2015), *Reflections on the Liar* (2017), and *Fictionalism in Philosophy* (co-edited with Fred Kroon, 2020).

Frederick Kroon

The University of Auckland

Frederick Kroon is Emeritus Professor of Philosophy at the University of Auckland. He has authored numerous papers in formal and philosophical logic, ethics, philosophy of language, and metaphysics, and is the author of *A Critical Introduction to Fictionalism* (with Stuart Brock and Jonathan McKeown-Green, 2018).

About the Series

This Cambridge Elements series provides an extensive overview of the many and varied connections between philosophy and logic. Distinguished authors provide an up-to-date summary of the results of current research in their fields and give their own take on what they believe are the most significant debates influencing research, drawing original conclusions.

Cambridge Elements ≡

Philosophy and Logic

Elements in the Series

Printed in the United States
by Baker & Taylor Publisher Services